# Taking Out The Trash

by:
s. y. shorter

*God Bless You
More & More!
Sharon Y. Shorter*

READY WRITER PUBLISHING

All scripture quotations, unless otherwise indicated, are taken from the New King James Version. Copyright © 1982 by Thomas Nelson, Inc. Used by permission. All rights reserved.

Scripture quotations marked (AMP) are taken from the Amplified Bible, Old Testament, copyright © 1965, 1987 by The Zondervan Corporation. The Amplified Bible, New Testament, copyright © 1954, 1958, 1987 by The Lockman Foundation. Used by permission.

Scripture quotations marked (CEV) are from the Contemporary English Version Copyright © 1991, 1992, 1995 by American Bible Society. Used by Permission.

Published by
READY WRITER PUBLISHING
P. O. Box 4281
Irving, Texas 75015

Copyright © 2002 by sharon y. shorter

All rights reserved. This book, or parts thereof, may not be reproduced in any form by any means-electronic, mechanical, photocopy, recording, or otherwise-without prior written permission of publisher, except provided by United States of America copyright law.

**Publishers Cataloging-in-Publication Data**:
Shorter, Sharon Y.
   Taking out the trash / by s. y. shorter.
   p. cm.
   ISBN: 0-9721721-3-0
   1. Man-woman relationships--Religious aspects--Christianity.
   2. Sex--Religious aspects--Christianity.
   3. Single people--Conduct of life.
   4. Mate selection--Religious aspects--Christianity. I. Title.
   BV4596.S5 S52 2002
       241.835-ddc21        2002092470

Printed in the United States of America
05 04 03 02 01  5 4 3 2 1

*Cover design by Devie Perry*

# Disclaimer

This book is designed to provide information in regard to the subject matters covered. It is sold with the understanding that the publisher and author are not engaged in rendering legal or professional services. If such assistance is required, the services of a competent professional should be sought.

The purpose of this book is to provide an informational resource tool. The author and Ready Writer Publishing shall have neither liability nor responsibility to any person or entity with respect to any loss or damage caused, or alleged to be caused, directly or indirectly by the information contained in this book.

If you do not wish to be bound by the above, you may return this book to the publisher for a full refund.

# Dedication

*After much pondering, I began to ask myself a few questions. That is who has impacted my life the most over the years. Who was the one person or persons who were most instrumental in changing my life and my view of life? For several days, I thought about what to say and to whom. Because most times the immediate response is a mother or father or very close relative, I kept coming back to the one person who has poured out and imparted into my life to the greatest degree. That one is a spiritual father who touched my heart most by his sincerity as a leader and a teacher.*

*He allowed me the opportunity to witness some of his most vulnerable moments through his transparency. These times were vivid pictures of the heart behind the man—a heart not only for his people but for all people. I saw mirror reflections of myself and the qualities that I desired to possess. His greatness is evident through his humility and I dedicate this book to "Pastor M. Hayes."*

# Contents

Epigraph ............................................................................... vi
Preface .................................................................................. vii

Introduction ........................................................................ 1

Emotional Enslavement ................................................... 5
*Food for Thought* .............................................................. 15

The Remedy ........................................................................ 17
*Food for Thought* .............................................................. 22

Choice Seed ........................................................................ 23
*Food for Thought* .............................................................. 28

Rocky Ground .................................................................... 29
*Food for Thought* .............................................................. 46

Fell By The Wayside ......................................................... 47
*Food for Thought* .............................................................. 74

Warning!!! Beware of Thorns ........................................ 77
*Food for Thought* .............................................................. 122

Some Fell On Good Ground .......................................... 125
*Food for Thought* .............................................................. 161

A Single Vessel Of Honor ............................................... 163
*Food for Thought* .............................................................. 169

A Dry Season ..................................................................... 171

Conclusion ......................................................................... 175

# Epigraph

§

"Have you ever wondered why you keep going from one bad relationship to another?

'Taking Out The Trash' is a book that will help to enlighten this matter. Yet it gives the insight to all who desire to grow in their relationship with the Lord Jesus Christ. The truths shared are simple, but equally profound. Everyone who will open their hearts and minds to the revelation shared in this book will receive healing and restoration from destructive patterns that we often find ourselves repeating.

This book will permanently change your life."

—*Prophetess Janice Hatten*

*He who receives a prophet in the name of a prophet shall receive a prophet's reward. And he who receives a righteous man in the name of a righteous man shall receive a righteous man's reward." (Matt. 10:41)*

# Preface

Oftentimes there are questions for which we may have no apparent answers. Many books can be informative and give reasons as to why one may find himself or herself in a consistent situation or circumstance in life. Valid reasons are given as to how someone gets from point A to what can be a very stagnant place in point B.

But in writing *Taking Out The Trash*, I want to take us a step further, by giving revelatory insight to and a release from an established pattern of poor choices in relationships.

I believe that most of our choices are based on our experiences. With the first experience of a relationship being with our parent(s), this will oftentimes influence our behaviors and our choices in future relationships with others. The impact of this delicate phase in life can leave behind many wounds and bruises.

The bruises are surfaced in many symptoms such as anger, low self-esteem, and rebellious acts of abuse and promiscuity. But the wounds are more deeply imbedded causing bitterness, resentment, and unforgiveness. This is the trash that so many of us collect along the road of life's experiences. And this is the trash we so desperately need to take out.

So, in order to bring a halt in the recycling process of generations of this trash, we must come to face many painstaking realities and understand that the relevant urgency for our recovery is finding the "Remedy."

# Introduction

§

Who could fault the humanistic side of us for desiring companionship in our lives? It is not uncommon to feel somewhat incomplete, especially without the bonding of another person. Often compounded with an overwhelming sense of loneliness, we search out relationships, as a means to an end. In essence, we look to the opposite sex, as well as to others, to meet our needs, when in actuality, there is only one source that can fill such a void.

Searching to find that common bond can become our most sought after task because the enemy has conspired with the world to convince us that our biological clocks are rapidly ticking away. It is of the utmost importance that

## Taking Out The Trash

this valuable time and attention be focused on the one who can be all things to all men and women, and that one is Jesus Christ.

There is not anything wrong with desiring companionship, but we often get ourselves caught up, tied up and tangled up. Oh, what a tangled web we can weave. Jeremiah 17:5 reads, "Thus *says the LORD: "Cursed is the man who trusts in man and makes flesh his strength, and whose heart departs from the LORD."*

Basically, God is saying that we are going to be faced with many troubles and disappointments, if we put our trust in man or woman, rather than in the Lord.

Time after time, we find ourselves disappointed by our friends and others because we put our trust in their ability to bring to us fulfillment and completion. We are apt to make them our main focus and that causes us to lose sight of the one whom has exactly what we need to become complete.

The aftermath of such misguided focus is an opened window for disappointments and brokenness. We become so vulnerable to the attacks of the enemy, because of the loneliness and this great sense of desperation to fill the

## Introduction

emptiness. The enemy immediately recognizes this void as a window of opportunity to slip in.

One avenue often used is to bring people into our lives that are not good to us and therefore are not good for us. So, we must learn to recognize the deceitful tactics of the enemy in whatever form they may appear. This is a key step towards freedom from situations and relationships that keep us in bondage.

Bondage subjects us to a power or influence that consumes our ability to function as confident, independent, self-controlled and emotionally stable people. Jesus said, *"And you shall know the truth, and the truth shall make you free." (John 8:32)*

So, we must get to know the one who is Truth, and also know the truth about our adversary.

The knowledge gained can release the bondages brought on through relationships that are unhealthy and not prosperous. With understanding, truth can bring the freedom that is so greatly desired, in the soul.

The soul is a reflection of life and life's experiences. It is out of the very depths of the soul that one responds to life.

## Taking Out The Trash

The soul can be fragile, yet sometimes stern. It is joyful, yet sometimes sorrowful (the emotions). It feels free, yet oftentimes is held captive (the will). It is renewed, yet often cluttered (the mind). Here is where we begin to take out the trash.

The soul reacts much like a sponge. It absorbs life. If not careful, the soul can become drenched even to the point of being submersed by life's experiences and it cannot function freely.

We will see how the souls of the men and women, who are depicted in the following chapters, are like sponges. Each will absorb from one another's experiences, because there are no boundaries or set limits to restrict the flow.

# 1
# Emotional Enslavement

§

We are often held captive by our emotions. The captivity is the result of the emotional enslavement that comes from relationships that are based on a deluded or a false sense of worthiness about one's self and the relationship. Delude refers to being deceived or mislead to the degree of not being able to detect falsehood or make sound judgement. Take Regina, whose false sense of worthiness hides behind the subconscious confirmations sought from others to conceal her lack of self-confidence.

Regina struggled with her weight most of her life. But she knew that somewhere (locked up) within, was a thin-little girl who desperately wanted to be set free. There

## Taking Out The Trash

was this little girl who wanted to feel love, acceptance and beautiful. But now, this same little girl has grown-up to be an adult woman, who still has these same desires.

There were many times that seem to fulfill Regina's most intimate wishes. Regina felt most secure when she was with someone special. It was these moments that made her feel the love and acceptance that she so desperately longed for. It was the emotional high that would give her such a rush that she would search to find that familiar place again, and again.

In her desperation and dependence on approval, she found Rod, who was not equipped with the foundation needed in order to build loving, kind and respectable relationships. An irrational and uncontrollable father had formed Rod's twisted perception of love.

Rod grew-up in an environment where the men were to always be the dominant figures. The man had to be in control of every situation, including his woman! Why was it so important to portray such a strong presence and have a dominant role? Because behind the strong man, there stood this little boy who needed love and affirmation from his own father. A little boy who wanted to express his deepest emotions but was told to never show his true

## Emotional Enslavement

feelings. And there was really never a need for true expression with Regina, because all she required was his presence.

Regina and Rod, who were without any spiritual discernment, were destined to meet. They became the blind leading the blind. Unfortunately, when the blind leads the blind, they fall into a ditch. Unable to recognize the truth, even the truth about themselves, has formed a false perception of self-worth. For Rod and Regina the ultimate truth, can only come with the self-admission of truth about themselves. Their release from their captivity can only be found in the mere searching of their shallow and incoherent souls, which consist of their minds, their wills and their emotions.

A soul, which lacks order and connection, falls out of harmony with the spirit of a man and ultimately out of harmony with the Spirit of God. The soul of a man has to be complete. The soul which is the mind, will and emotions must be one (connected) with the spirit, which seeks to be one with the Spirit of God.

Similar circumstances shapes Kathleen's life. This past and present ghost of co-dependency continues to haunt her life. Out of fear of being alone, co-dependency has drained the independent life, right out of her being.

# Taking Out The Trash

Kathleen, who never had much opportunity to be by herself, loved being in a family environment. This was her comfort zone. Even as a small child, Kathleen thought of having her own family. Unfortunately, her wish came true much sooner than expected. Burden with the responsibility to care for her father, who was physically disabled, Kathleen deeply resented him for her lack of independence. She thought, "If I could only get away, then I could be free." But who would she be free from? Yes, she would be free from her father, but she would forever be held captive by her own inward fear of being alone.

Kathleen would eventually leave home in search of her freedom but only to realize the freedom, in which she searched for, was no where to be found. There was a constant need to have someone around to care for and she truly hated the thought of being by herself. What was causing such a reluctance to being alone? Kathleen always had the responsibility of taking care of everything and everybody, so there was a fear of not being needed. And she was not sure of her ability to function in any other capacity.

We will find that Kathleen's life is shaped by an addiction of co-dependency with people. She is addicted to people like John, who can trust no one. As a young boy, John

## Emotional Enslavement

was very angry. He was angry with both his mother and father for not having the ideal marital relationship. John watched his father drink excessively but amazingly his father still managed to keep his job. John wasn't sure how his father could remain faithful to his mother because of the many secrets that plague their household.

John's perception of women had been unconsciously framed by his mother's adulterous lifestyle. Why did he believe that all women were not worthy to be trusted? Because of the lack of trust in John's family, he lived with resentment for his mother and the fear of hurt and shame. Somehow his will to trust had been restrained. Yet, because of a deep desire to truly believe in another, his will would secretly cry out for its freedom.

But there is Bobby, who Kathleen views as somewhat trusting, but who happens to be an occasional user. The question is, can Kathleen really trust him or even trust herself? Because of the bond between these two, they ultimately become one, as Kathleen's life somehow seems to become absorbed by Bobby's co-dependency with drugs. As a result, their souls (mind, will and emotions) would become trapped within this web of co-dependencies.

## Taking Out The Trash

The road to freedom for Kathleen, John and Bobby is on the pathway to truth. The truth comes in freedom from each other and their addictions.

Without order, an unrestrained soul can be filled with many uncontrollable urges and addictions. Jade would find this to be very true. In her own efforts to find fulfillment, she practiced irrational and unhealthy, but learned behaviors. Why did Jade's actions and reactions feel so normal? An imbedded pattern of attitudes and values led Jade to continue her mother's promiscuous lifestyle.

Jade became sexually active at an early age. The idea of having sex was planted in Jade's mind when she accidentally found her mother's pornographic magazine hidden beneath the mattress. She often fantasized about this experience. Jade watched her mother go and come with many different men and this sparked her curiosity. Jade not only viewed sex as a pass-time but also as a means to getting whatever she desired.

The irony of the deception that ruled her life gave reason to justify her irresponsible behaviors. Sex became a bargaining tool in which Jade had no control. As a result, Jade made Randy a grand offer, he had to refuse.

## Emotional Enslavement

Randy, who was committed to a lifestyle of celibacy, was even deceived into thinking that his clock was rapidly ticking away.

Randy, who experienced marriage and divorce more than a few times, saw several close family members go through this tragedy. At age twelve his parents were divorced. So Randy desperately wanted his next marriage to last forever. He wanted to trust God for the right relationship. But because God was not moving fast enough, Randy sought to take matters into his own hands to choose the one who he wanted, rather than waiting for the one who he needed.

Randy's emotional instability caused him to become overly anxious. The loneliness opened up the door and allowed the deceit to step in. His soul lacked the connection and order he needed to follow his spirit. He became dissatisfied with feelings of hopelessness and worthlessness. Randy would find himself being led by his emotions rather than by his spirit. Because his soul was desperate for a connection, whether it was positive or negative, Jade responded and the two became drawn to one another.

Why did Randy have such an attraction to someone like Jade? The attraction stemmed from a false sense of

# Taking Out The Trash

connection and order. Proverbs 27:7 says, *"A satisfied soul loathes the honeycomb, But to a hungry soul every bitter thing is sweet."* What does this mean? A satisfied soul greatly dislikes what is honeycombed with lies and deceit, but to a dissatisfied soul every bitter thing is sweet and seems to be the right connection. Proverbs 9:17 says, *"Stolen water is sweet, And bread eaten in secret is pleasant."* When the soul is not in order with the spiritual things of God, it seeks out what is hidden and forbidden. So, in order to have the right connection, we have to take out the trash.

Because our emotions are our sensibility to things, situations and people, we may say that we do not want the kind of relationship our parents had but we may unknowingly seek out people just like them. Determined not to fall into this horrible pit, Crystal refused to be controlled by anyone, especially men. She abhorred the thought of being in a relationship like that of her parents. If the right man reminded Crystal of her father then he instantly became the wrong man. So why did every man turn out to be the wrong man in Crystal's life? Because of her emotional entrapment, she was unable to make sound judgement about the people who came into her life.

Crystal's only picture of marriage was that of her father verbally and physically abusing her mother. The lingering

## Emotional Enslavement

anger and unforgiveness stemming from her relationship with her father caused Crystal to push everyone out and shut herself in. Trapped by her very own emotions, she avoided getting too close because of fear, hurt and rejection.

Unfortunately, Derek got the opportunity to experience some of Crystal's pain. This only compounded his very own wounds. Derek thought he was over the hurt from his divorce, but he really was an accident waiting to happen. Derek suffered severe internal bleeding. How could this be? Because on the surface, he appeared to be healed but the scars from the betrayal of his wife was so much deeper. Shortly after marriage, Derek's wife left him for another man. So, he vowed to never be taken advantage of again and he made that very clear.

Many of us have gone through similar experiences that have left behind a wounded and bruised soul. The bruises are on the surface but the wounds go much deeper. Our lives are often left cluttered with this trash because of past experiences and dysfunctional childhoods. This is the trash that so desperately needs to be discarded in order to build good and healthy relationships. The rejection, resentment, hurt, anger, bitterness and unforgiveness seem to govern our entire beings and to all of which we

# Taking Out The Trash

become hostages. It is the vile odor from this trash that turns God's face away in sorrow and grieves the Holy Spirit from within.

Our past relationships with friends and family, especially with parents, can greatly impact our future relationships with others. Until the ones, who are left broken by these past experiences, allow Jesus Christ to come into their lives and clean out the trash, they are destined to repeat these same broken patterns over and over again in future relationships.

Regardless of how broken one may be, Jesus Christ will accept all the broken pieces and begin to put them back together. Jesus wants you to be in the right relationship, but this begins by being in the right relationship with Him. Right now, you can accept Him, because He has already accepted you, just as you are. Allow Him to repair and prepare your heart to receive the promise of God. The promise of an abundant life of love, peace, joy and fulfillment in and through Jesus Christ.

Emotional Enslavement

## Food For Thought

- A soul, which lacks order and connection, falls out of harmony with the spirit of a man and ultimately out of harmony with the Spirit of God.

- The mind, will and emotions must be one (connected) with the spirit, which seeks to be one with the Spirit of God.

- The road to freedom is on the pathway to truth.

- Without order, an unrestrained soul can be filled with many uncontrollable urges and addictions.

- A satisfied (full) soul greatly dislikes what is honeycombed (covered) with lies and deceit. But to a dissatisfied (empty) soul every bitter thing is sweet and seems to be the right connection.

- Life experiences can leave behind a wounded and bruised soul.

- The trash (unforgiveness, rebellion, resentment, anger, bitterness and etc.) must be discarded in order to build good and healthy relationships.

- Until we allow Jesus Christ to take out the trash, we are destined to repeat the same broken patterns over and over in future relationships.

# Taking Out The Trash

# 2
# The Remedy

§

The Word of God instructs us, *"But seek first the kingdom of God and His righteousness, and all these things shall be added to you." (Matt. 6:33)* All things include fulfillment and completion that only comes in and through Jesus Christ.

So, we can trust God for all things including our soul mates. Trust is the most essential part of a relationship. Trust is having the confidence in someone's integrity, character, and ability. The Bible says that we are blessed when we trust in Jesus Christ. And if we are trusting in Him, then how much of our time and attention is being focused on trying to find the right person or the right connection?

# Taking Out The Trash

Our time is so valuable and should be treasured. *"For where your treasure is, there your heart will be also." (Matt. 6:21)* This means where your time (treasure) is directed, your heart will be focused there also.

Your treasure is whatever or whomever you invest a vast amount of time in. So, consider whether or not that person in your life or that person in your mind has consumed all of your time and your focus. Has he or she become your treasure? Because of where and in whom you place your treasure, there your heart will be directed. Jesus' desire is to have your time, especially your heart because He treasures your trust in Him. Could it be that the hurt and the many disappointments in life have caused a lack of trust and your heart has turned away from God?

Many failed attempts in relationships can lead to mistrust and can even cause bitterness toward God. God understands our wounds and He acknowledges our need for healing. *"For the heart of this people has grown dull. Their ears are hard of hearing and their eyes they have closed, lest they should see with their eyes and hear with their ears, lest they should understand with their heart and turn, so that I should heal them." (Matt. 13:15)* The Lord expresses himself as a Father who desires to bring

## The Remedy

comfort and healing to the hurting. As Jehovah-rophe, He is the God who heals. The name alone signifies Jehovah as the healer.

The first chapter of the book of Isaiah conveys God's heart to heal His people. Yet the remedy relies on the willingness and the obedience of the sick and the wounded to receive it. God spoke of the children of Israel whom he had brought up and nourished, but they had responded to Him in rebellion. What a sense of rejection!

How is it, that an ox instinctively knows his owner and a donkey knows his master's crib but the children of Israel did not recognize or understand, nor would even consider the God who fathered them. As a result of Israel's sinful nature, they had forsaken the Lord, provoked Him to anger and turned their hearts away.

Israel had a desperate and urgent need for a physician and this was evident in Isaiah 1:5,6. The Lord said, *"Why should you be stricken again? You will revolt more and more. The whole head is sick, and the whole heart faints. From the sole of the foot even to the head, there is no soundness in it, but wounds and bruises and putrefying sores; they have not been closed or bound up, or soothed with ointment."* These wounds were even felt in God's compassion for his people in the book of Jeremiah.

# Taking Out The Trash

Jeremiah, the Prophet, conveyed God's heart felt sorrow stemming from a longing desire to heal His children. God expressed, *"For the hurt of the daughter of my people I am hurt. I am mourning; astonishment has taken hold of me. Is there no balm in Gilead, is there no physician there? Why then is there no recovery for the health of the daughter of my people?" (Jer. 8:21,22)*

What a God of compassion who desired to be their Jehovah-rophe, the God who heals? Has not one, even sought to recognize, understand, or even to consider the Remedy? If you are wounded from past hurts and in need of a physician, seek Him, the Remedy.

God wants to heal you and bring you into the fullness of His glory. He wants to bring you into right relationship with Him. Jesus Christ's desire is to heal the brokenhearted and to bind up their wounds. He wants to bring you out of darkness into the marvelous light, so that you can see and recognize the one who brings truth. When you can identify the enemy and his tactics, he cannot defeat or destroy God's divine purpose for your abundant life. *"The thief does not come except to steal, and to kill, and to destroy. I have come that they may have life, and that they may have it more abundantly." (John 10:10)* The

## The Remedy

abundant life, which is promised to you, is filled with love, peace and joy. Jesus Christ died for us and because of His blood, which was shed on the cross, we are now healed of the wounds and therefore, released from the pain. Jesus loves you so much, that in your place, He has already suffered the hurts and the bruises that life can bring.

Jesus Christ assures us that He is the good shepherd and His sheep follows Him for they know His voice. *"My sheep hear My voice, and I know them, and they follow Me." (John 10:27)* Right now, Jesus is speaking to your heart to follow after Him. If you would hear, Jesus would say to you, "I want to fill that hollow place. I want to fill that void which no one seems to satisfy or will ever satisfy."

Satisfaction is not always guaranteed. Especially when our investment is sown into others with the expectation of receiving a great return. We invest time, money and words without considering that there are risks, obstacles, setbacks and other forces that can hinder the amount of return on our investments. Satisfaction is not always guaranteed, except when we invest in Jesus Christ, who is the Remedy.

# Taking Out The Trash

## Food For Thought

- *Trust in the most essential part of a relationship.*

- *Your treasure is whatever or whomever you invest a vast amount of time in.*

- *The remedy relies on the willingness and the obedience of the sick and the wounded to receive it.*

- *Has not one, even sought to recognize, understand, or even consider the "Remedy?"*

- *If you are wounded from past hurts and in need of a physician, seek Him, the "Remedy."*

- *When you can identify the enemy and his tactics, he cannot defeat or destroy God's devine purpose for your abundant life.*

- *Jesus Christ wants to fill the void that no one seems to satisfy nor will ever satisfy.*

- *Satisfaction is not always guaranteed, except when we invest in Jesus Christ who is the "Remedy."*

# 3
# Choice Seed

§

In the parable of the sower: Luke 8:5-8 (AMP), *"A sower went out to sow seed; and as he sowed, some fell along the traveled path and was trodden underfoot, and the birds of the air ate it up. And some [seed] fell on the rock, and as soon as it sprouted, it withered away because it had no moisture. And other [seed] fell in the midst of the thorns, and the thorns grew up with it and choked it [off]. And some seed fell into the good soil, and grew up and yielded a crop a hundred times [as great]. As He said these things, He called out, He who has ears to hear, let him be listening and let him consider and understand by hearing!"*

# Taking Out The Trash

What is the Holy Spirit saying, right now? If you want a hundred percent return, that is satisfaction guaranteed, then invest in Me. The value of our return has a lot to do with the choices we make. A farmer who goes out to plant a crop must not only consider the type of seed but the type of ground needed to produce a great harvest.

Which sower are you? Are you planting seeds (time, money and the Word of God) in good soil, in order to bear good fruit or are you wasting your time picking one bad apple after another? The Bible states that whatever we sow, that we will also reap. If we sow into the flesh, we will of the flesh reap corruption. This same principle applies when we sow into the Spirit.

How can we expect to reap the spiritual promises of God when the Spirit is not our choice of seed nor ground?

**Our choice of seed has to be of a God nature, sown into ground that has a God disposition, in order to produce God promises.**

What about the choices made by Regina, Kathleen, Jade and Crystal? How might their choices have been affected? These are women who are trying to find fulfillment in relationships with chosen men, who like themselves have lived dysfunctional lives since childhood. How can we

## Choice Seed

relate to men like Rod, John, Bobby and Randy who are broken in heart and in spirit? They are all people who are looking for love and happiness in all the wrong places. Men and women who are desperately seeking the path of completion for their lives but via the wrong means which is through others. They are men and women who as small children grew up in the church. Most went willingly, while others went only out of family tradition.

Even now, Regina finds herself in church; if she cannot come up with an excuse good enough to convince herself to stay home this Sunday. Kathleen, who does go to church quite regularly, at least twice a month, finds that she can really get into the music. However, Jade is being constantly invited by a friend and responds by saying, "Girl, if it's the Lord's will, I'll be there." Jade, who has now gotten tired of being asked, decides that she will go occasionally. On the other hand, Crystal had stopped going to church for a while but began to feel that something was missing in her life. She was reminded how, as a little girl, she always attended church on Sunday.

Just as important are the men, whom these women become involved with, because they also have experienced a few shuffles in life. Unfortunately for the men, as well as the women, they all are blinded by the cares of this world and are in a fight with themselves and the blows of life. Their lives are now being governed by the choices which they have made. Ironically, what has shaped their lives are those very same choices.

Our lives are structured by our choices. We make good choices and we make bad ones. We make bad choices even when we know that they are bad. With every choice comes the by-product of consequences. Our lives reflect the consequences of our choices and some of our parent's choices. Our parents made a decision to have sex, which produced a seed that produced a child. Further decisions were made about how to raise up the child. Through this process came our life experiences which almost always influences our future choices.

Remember the things we experience as children greatly effect our adult life. If we are taught as children to make sound choices, then as grown-ups, we are inclined to do the same. Not to say, we will never make a wrong decision but there is some comfort in knowing that when you *"Train up a child in the way he should go, And when he is old he will not depart from it." (Prov. 22:6)*

So, why do we make the choices that we do? Most of our decisions are based on our experiences and the knowledge which we gain from those experiences.

## Choice Seed

In looking into the lives of these four women and the men whom they encounter, we will find that something or someone in the past has caused their hearts to harden to the Word of God, causing them to continually make the same choices.

Taking Out The Trash

# Food For Thought

- *The value of our return has a lot to do with the choices we make.*

- *Our choice of seed has to be of a God nature, sown into ground that has a God disposition, in order to produce God promises.*

- *With every choice comes the by-product of consequences.*

- *Our lives reflect the consequences of our choices and some of our parent's choices.*

- *The things that we experience as children greatly effect our adult life.*

- *Most of our decisions are based on our experiences and the knowledge which we gain from those experiences.*

# 4
# Rocky Ground

§

Recall in the "parable of the sower," that while Jesus was sitting in the boat and as he began to speak, the crowd gathered around the shore. At that moment, Jesus revealed what the parable meant. Matthew, Mark and Luke each gave their own account of this event. The seed represents the Word of God. The seeds that fell by the wayside are those who hear the Word, but the devil or the enemy comes and take the message away from their hearts, in order to keep them from receiving the free gift of salvation. The enemy immediately snatches the Word away so that there is no revelation of salvation or manifestation of divine truth.

# Taking Out The Trash

The seeds that fell on rocky ground stand for those who hear the Word and are excited about receiving it. Unfortunately the Word does not take root and therefore, the Word does not sink deep into their heart. When the time of trial or temptation comes, they fall away from God and give up. The Word, which is the foundation, is not solid in them but instead is one that wavers with the forces that come against it.

The seeds that fell among thorn bushes are the ones who hear the Word and proceed to go out into the world. But because of pride and greed, they are choked or overtaken by the deceitfulness of riches, along with the cares and pleasures of life. These are the ones whose seeds become unfruitful. The breath of life received from the Word of God is cut off by the pleasures of this world and this causes the seed (Word) not to produce its potential hundred-fold harvest.

The seeds that fell on good ground stand for those who hear the Word and retain it in a good and obedient heart. They keep the Word in their hearts (good ground) and persist until they produce fruit with patience. The Word is kept in their hearts until it manifests itself into reality in the form of salvation, deliverance, healing and the many blessings of God.

## Rocky Ground

Which sower are you? Are you receiving God's word in good ground (your heart) and producing a fruitful harvest with obedience and patience? Otherwise, your seeds may be falling by the wayside, on rocky ground or even among thorn bushes. A fruitful (plentiful) harvest requires the seed to be fertilized in good ground with obedience and patience.

Patience involves waiting on the right timing. Everything happens in God's perfect timing. Even developing good and healthy relationships require waiting on God to place the right people into our lives. In essence, patience is formed through standing on God's word that he will supply all of our needs, emotionally, physically, and spiritually. God wants us to depend on Him totally, by fully expecting Him to direct our path. This includes directing the right people into our lives who are spiritually aligned with His word. 2 Corinthians 6:14 states, *"Do not be unequally yoked together with unbelievers. For what fellowship has righteousness with lawlessness? And what communion has light with darkness?"*

When does the wisdom come in making good choices? We should come into relationship with men and women who are spiritually in tune with God. Someone who is responding to the promptings of the Holy Spirit and is led by Him. We should allow the Holy Spirit to lead in every

## Taking Out The Trash

aspect of our lives, including developing long-term relationships. If we prayerfully ask and patiently wait, God will bring that special someone into our existence by placing him or her into our path.

By no means shall we women seek to find husbands. God has given this privilege to the man. *"He who finds a wife finds a good thing, And obtains favor from the LORD." (Prov. 18:22)* Sometimes our nature, as women, is to become overly anxious and to move out of order. So, let us not rob the man of his position nor his opportunity to obtain divine favor. This will not only benefit the man, but the wife, as well.

But like many of us who live in the here and now world, we want what we want today, not tomorrow or sometime in the future. Have you ever given much thought as to why you choose the companionships or friendships that you choose?

Remember Regina? She is one of those women who is looking for love and happiness in all the wrong places. For instance, she is unaware that she has low self-esteem. It's like developing cancer and having not yet been diagnosed, and until you become aware that the problem exists, it gets worse or may even be fatal.

# Rocky Ground

Regina has faced some of the same problems since childhood. A constant battle with her weight seemed never-ending. She always wanted to fit in with the crowd, but she never really did. She thought if she catered to the needs of others, then in turn, they would do the same for her. Do you find yourself like Regina who is always seeking approval or confirmation from someone else? Do you look to Rod, Eric and Danny for constant reminders that you are pretty, that you smell good and that you are wanted? Do you give in to the simple, but nice and sweet compliments from him? Even though you are not attracted to him nor interested in him, but the fact that he knows the right things to say, you reluctantly give in anyway.

If there is not someone there saying these things to you at all times, you feel empty and undesirable. So, you unknowingly seek out whoever may fill this void in your life.

Like Regina, who finds herself dating guys whose sole purpose is just to get what they can get, while the getting is good. She even goes without paying her rent or utilities, if Eric feels he needs a new outfit for the weekend. Only surprisingly enough, Regina is not the one who he is taking out.

## Taking Out The Trash

Then Danny comes along with his smooth talk and he doesn't feel like riding the local bus today. So, he wants to borrow the car. It's just for a couple of hours and he'll be right back. Well, Regina thinks to herself, "It's only for a few hours. What could it hurt? Besides, he makes me feel good and if I don't, he will never call me again."

Somehow, Danny forgot his watch and could not tell what time of the day it was. A couple of hours turned into sun-up to sundown or maybe even into the next day. Perhaps he fell asleep over at his sister's house on the couch, and she forgot to awaken him. Therefore, you received no phone call.

Let's not mention that you just bought a spanking, brand new, candy-apple red convertible Mustang. You even made sure the dealer threw in a digital display of the time, which is conveniently placed on the dash. So, there is no excuse for the time thing.

Rod, on the other hand, does have a car and a job. Regina is very impressed with this one. After all, for someone who is tall, dark and handsome to be with her, he must really care. Regina saw Rod as a man who feared nothing or no one. This reminded her of growing up and her father who was tall, thin and somewhat of a forceful man. All he

## Rocky Ground

had to do was to be present and everything was in order. But her dad sometimes went away for days at a time. Regina recalls lying awake at night wondering where he could be. He would return home quietly in the night. Regretfully, being questioned by her mother, only to bring about a rage of anger from her father, which resulted in unimaginative physical and verbal abuse.

Regina thought to herself, "Rod reminds me of my father when he gets angry. Maybe like my mother, I am somehow responsible. Maybe, if I had not questioned his whereabouts for the past three days, he would not have gotten so upset with me."

Surprisingly, Rod's little three-day vacation was spent just across town with a friend, Regina's friend.

What prompted Rod's unpredictable behavior? Rod's actions and reactions stem from being in the presence of his father, who ruled and dominated everything and everybody. No one was to ever question his father's decisions or his father's whereabouts. Under no circumstance was anyone ever allowed to voice their opinion unless he or she was asked.

Unbeknown to him, Rod was being programmed to act and respond just like his father. Mirroring his father's

# Taking Out The Trash

actions, Rod had no regards for the feelings of the women who were in his life. Ironically, Rod thought this was how he should show love. Besides, his mother always seemed very happy no matter what his father did or said. Rod rationalized that all women were to be just as happy, like his mother. If a woman had his presence, what more could she possibly ask for?

Needless to say, the things we experience as children can greatly affect our responses to others. As a child, Rod had not experienced the beauty of true love in the relationship between his mother and father. Rod was not equipped with the foundation needed in order to build loving, kind, and respectful relationships. But as an adult man, there is hope for Rod.

The hope we have in Jesus Christ who gives instructions in his Word on how to love, specifically the love of a husband for his wife. Christ exemplifies this love for His bride, which we know as the church. By surrendering to God and following God's example and His instructions, Rod can develop prosperous relationships, enriched with the love of Jesus Christ.

Rod's image of a husband and wife relationship has to be recreated to reflect that of Jesus Christ's vision for His

# Rocky Ground

bride. Ephesians emphasizes the love that Jesus Christ has for the church as the same love a husband should have for his wife: (Ephesians 5:25,28,29)

> *Verse 25: "Husbands, love your wives, just as Christ also loved the church and gave Himself for it".*
> *Verse 28: "So husbands ought to love their own wives as their own bodies; he who loves his wife loves himself."*
> *Verse 29: "For no one ever hated his own flesh, but nourishes and cherishes it, just as the Lord does the church."*

Most often the one person, whom we will nourish, respect and take great care of, is one's self. A man, who loves his wife, loves himself. The way we see ourselves and the way we feel about ourselves are often reflected in our responses to others. It is impossible for a man to give to his wife or to his children what he does not have to give. So, how might one receive this fervent love, which Jesus Christ expresses for His bride? The Bible teaches us how to love unconditionally. Jesus commands us to love our neighbor, as ourselves. Sometimes the most difficult part is the loving of one's self. "As yourself" references to the same degree. You can only love your neighbor to the same degree that you love yourself.

# Taking Out The Trash

The process begins when we accept the love of Jesus Christ. We cannot give to others what we have not yet received. God so loved the world that He gave his only begotten son. God sacrificed His son, so that you can receive the love of Jesus Christ. This unconditional love can't be given, until it has been received through the acceptance of Jesus Christ. Only then can this love be freely given, as it was freely received. This love cost us nothing but cost Jesus Christ everything.

Seeking to be in relationship with Jesus is the first step to having a loving relationship that leads to a loving marriage. Rod has to develop a relationship with Jesus Christ. He must ask for forgiveness and also forgive those who have hurt him. This is the beginning of the promise of an abundant life.

By accepting Jesus Christ as his personal Savior and allowing God to take out the trash, he eliminates the blockage, thus opening up a vessel that can receive the unconditional love and blessings of the Lord. This is the kind of love that is transferable to others.

What can we gain from Rod's life experiences? We know that all of the old and negative mindsets and learned behaviors must be discarded. We can trust God to prepare us for the greatest relationship of all with Him. Self-love

## Rocky Ground

not selfish love begins with Jesus Christ. God wants to be first and foremost in our lives. We must plant good seeds into good ground to produce a great harvest. Our seeds are God's word, our time, our finances and our love. We can determine our harvest by our choice of seed, and the ground, in which we choose to plant. Remember the frost, the wind, the rain will come but not destroy the harvest that God has promised to produce from the seed which falls on to good ground.

So, our challenge is not to allow our seed to fall onto rocky ground. The seeds that fell on rocky ground stand for those who hear the Word and receive it gladly but the Word does not take root in their hearts. They believe for a while but when the temptation comes, they fall away from God and give up. In order to be secure and to stand the test of adversity, the Word must sink deep into our hearts. The Word has to become the solid foundation.

What causes someone to be drawn away from God? Why was Regina drawn to a man like Rod? Remember that she has heard the Word of God constantly from friends and family but she had often pulled away.

Regina receives the Word with pleasure but it does not take root in her heart. She believes God's will for her life,

# Taking Out The Trash

but as soon as satan comes on as the smooth operator, she falls away.

Why? Because we are drawn away from God by the fulfillment of our own selfish desires. Our defense is to recognize the deceitful and luring tactics of the enemy, whether it is in a blue or black suit.

The Word has to penetrate into Regina's heart. The issues that Regina faces, low self-esteem, feelings of rejection is the trash that hinders her from receiving a great harvest. Our soil becomes contaminated and the seed cannot take root. Even good seed, like the Word of God requires good soil in order to produce its potential hundred-fold return.

Remember there are forces that want to hinder the return on our investment. Once the seeds are sown into our heart, the test and obstacles that come to us are designed to bring forth patience. The return comes in the form of perseverance and patience to wait on God for the harvest.

In Luke's account of the parable of the sower, as soon as the seed fell on rocky ground, it sprung up, dried, and withered away because there was no moisture. We will immediately give up (wither) because the Word has not been rooted in our heart. There is no substance or depth

## Rocky Ground

(word or perseverance) within to draw strength from, in order to maintain life and to grow. Therefore, we wither away. The devil comes to steal, kill and destroy our harvest and our lives.

A deep-seeded Word (seed) has to be watered and nourished through a personal relationship with Jesus Christ. This is the same apparent truth that operates in a parent and child relationship. The child, who is the parent's seed, must be watered and nourished, in order to grow. The child's growth stems from a personal and healthy relationship with the parent(s). Therefore, our spiritual growth depends on a personal and healthy relationship with Jesus Christ.

Regardless of our fragmented past, we must not give up, for there is hope. The hope is in Jesus Christ. God wants us to know that approval is not necessary from others to know that we are worthy and precious to Him. He wants you to know that you are uniquely made in His likeness. In spite of the brokenness, God has never made an error. He created you for a purpose. Your purpose is to complete the plan God has for your life. You are a part of God's glorious plan for a glorious Kingdom, because there is no mistake in a Master's plan.

## Taking Out The Trash

Each one of us possesses unique and individual qualities. Begin to say to yourself, "I am God's workmanship and through Jesus Christ all things are possible. I am complete in Christ. I am the apple of my Father's eye and He loves me with an everlasting love that assures me that He will supply all my need according to His riches in glory by Jesus Christ."

Before we can love someone else, we must love ourselves. We must love the person whom God created us to be. Learning to accept ourselves as the ones, who God created in His likeness, will allow us to walk in His image as children of the King. As heirs to royalty, we are entitled to all the benefits of royalty. Royalty doesn't need approval from anyone. Once we know [that we know] who we are, the only confirmation needed is from the King, himself.

Jesus Christ died so that you may have life—an abundant life and eternal life. You can now walk in completeness, confidence, holiness and in contentment in the presence of the Most High God.

God has taken out the trash of low self-esteem, anger, bitterness, resentment and the heartbreak resulting from a broken past. He has cleansed and healed you by the blood of Jesus Christ, the Anointed One and His anointing. Repentance allows God to begin to take out the trash.

## Rocky Ground

Matthew 6:33 says, *"But seek first the kingdom of God and His righteousness, and all these things shall be added to you."*

Remember, while seeking God first and waiting on Him to add all these things to you, patience is of the utmost importance. Patience is going through difficult times, including times of loneliness, with calm endurance while not complaining or losing self control.

*"Our soul waits for the LORD; He is our help and our shield. For our heart shall rejoice in Him, Because we have trusted in His holy name." (Psalm 33:20,21)* We must trust God to complete the process of taking out the trash.

Trusting God requires developing patience. A lesson on patience can prove to be very valuable. Some Greek definitions of patience include being hopeful, cheerful, consistent, and having endurance while waiting. One thing we all may be guilty of is saying, "Lord give me patience." When we ask God for patience, He will give it but not the way we think or would like for Him to. It won't be fast, quick and in a hurry or by some supernatural insemination. God will allow us to go through trials, which will teach us to have patience or perseverance.

## Taking Out The Trash

James, who was a servant of God, tells us that we can profit from the trials that we encounter in life.

*(James 1: 2-4) "My brethren, count it all joy when you fall into various trials, knowing that the testing of your faith produces patience. But let patience have its perfect work, that you may be perfect and complete, lacking nothing."*

As a result of patience, we become perfect and complete and lacking nothing. Our souls become satisfied. Sounds like satisfaction guaranteed. When we develop patience, we will wait on God and He will reward to us the life, which He has promised to those who love Him. Remember that every good and perfect gift comes from above. God has the perfect mate for you. Pray and ask God for the person whom He has anointed and appointed for you and then wait on Him, not him or her.

*(Psalm 40: 1) "I WAITED patiently for the LORD; And He inclined to me, And heard my cry."*

God wants us to be perfect and complete, and lacking nothing.This includes having that special someone who is emotionally, physically and spiritually compatible to us and will enhance the areas where we may be weak, but not lacking.

## Rocky Ground

While waiting on God and believing for what you have asked, start to spend time getting to know your Father. In order to get to know someone, you must spend time with that person. A personal relationship with Jesus Christ requires that same commitment. You can begin by ministering to Him and serving Him. This is the perfect time to really study the Word of God, read inspirational books, and listen to spiritual teachings to encourage yourself.

By keeping your eyes on the plan, it takes your eyes off the man or woman. Who has the plan? God does.

> *(Jeremiah 29: 11-13) "For I know the thoughts that I think toward you,' says the LORD, 'thoughts of peace and not evil, to give you a future and a hope. 'Then you will call upon Me and go and pray to Me, and I will listen to you. 'And you will seek Me and find Me, when you search for Me with all your heart."*

# Taking Out The Trash

## Food For Thought

- *The seeds that Fell On Rocky Ground are those who hear and are excited, but the Word does not sink deep into their hearts.*

- *Trash can contaminate our soil and the seeds cannot take root.*

- *The way we see ourselves and the way we feel about ourselves are often reflected in our responses to others.*

- *Unbeknowned to us, we can be programmed to act and respond just like our parents.*

- *Unconditional love cannot be given, until it has been received through the acceptance of Jesus Christ who is love.*

- *A fruitful (plentiful) harvest requires the seed to be fertilized in good ground with obedience and patience.*

- *As a result of patience, we become perfect and complete and lacking nothing.*

# 5
# Fell By The Wayside

§

One of the greatest desires of mankind is to feel loved. Love is often viewed as a subjective expression. If the subjectiveness is given to an individual's own personal experience, what determines our perception of true love? Love affects the part of the soul that yearns for companionship and affection. Our emotions are our sensibility to things, situations and people. The emotions are the part of the soul, which seeks to find a connection. We want to feel that we belong. Whether it is to an organization, club or someone, it gives us a sense of belonging or a sense of importance. The security in belonging takes away the feeling of loneliness. In the book of Joshua, God offers us an everlasting and faithful

## Taking Out The Trash

companion. God's word assures us that He will always be there, because He will never leave us nor forsake us.

The soul has a deep desire to belong. The fear that comes from not having this connection can create a handicap. Being alone can become debilitating for some and can even give them a sense of inadequacy. The constant desire to feel needed will sometimes lead an individual to physical and emotional states of co-dependency.

Co-dependency can occur as a result of a poor relationship with family or friends. Poor might indicate that the relationship is under nurtured and imbalanced. Some may even lack in individuality. One or more persons may often feel lost or incomplete without the presence of the other(s). Two of the greatest challenges for people who are co-dependent are the acceptance of themselves and being independent of others.

We must first love ourselves before we can love anyone else. Co-dependency can evolve from low self-esteem. It can lead to unstable and unsafe relationships. A person, who is co-dependent, main purpose is to please others. There is an irresistible impulse to always take responsibility for the other person's actions and choices. Some co-dependents resist being independent and are at times unable to take care of themselves. Due to the

## Fell By The Wayside

constant focus on the needs of others and the inability to make sound decisions, co-dependents often find it difficult to achieve goals of their own.

Also, someone may have been forced to become overly independent at a very early age. As a result, the need to always be in the position of caretaker can also create a one-sided relationship. Still the person's main focus is to fulfill the desires and expectations of others. Because much of a co-dependent's time and attention is directed toward others, they often lose sight of their own personal feelings and needs.

Co-dependency is an addiction. An addiction can be physiological and/or psychological. The compulsion is to obsessively devoted or habitually surrender to something or someone. Co-dependents are addicted to people or situations that provide an unhealthy atmosphere or surrounding for them. This addiction can result in making poor choices in relationships, as well as in life.

Women, as well as men, can sometimes develop patterns of making poor choices in relationships. This may occur time after time until the reasons, as to why, are determined. Co-dependents who are addicted to people feel that there has to be someone or a significant other, at all times, in their life. He or she may go from one

## Taking Out The Trash

relationship immediately into another for fear of being alone. Usually, they go from one bad relationship to another.

We can recognize the tracks of co-dependency in the past and present stages of Kathleen's life. She proves to be the perfect example of someone who goes from one bad situation to another. Because of her strong desire for marriage, she settled for what seemed to be the next best thing. And that was to be in relationships that seem to offer a long-term commitment.

Immediately following seven years of abuse, Kathleen began searching for a replacement. By going in and out of many relationships, her life seemed much like a revolving door.

Kathleen's greatest fear was being by herself. She continually thought, "How can I possibly survive alone?" John was Kathleen's backbone and her support mechanism. She feared the opportunity to function alone and hated the thought of it.

Even though Kathleen was smart and attractive, her confidence became shy and hidden. Her lack of ambition led to great dependency on John. While her whole life had been centered on pleasing him, everything and everyone

## Fell By The Wayside

else was of no significance. Kathleen's own needs and desires were often left unattended.

John, on the other hand, was a take charge individual with a controlling spirit. He exercised complete control over Kathleen's life, even to the point of threatening her. Kathleen feared freedom as much as she feared John. She was horrified and immobilized by John's constant threats. She knew there could be only one reason for John's outrageous and jealous behavior. He often recalled as a young boy, his mother entertaining many different men while his father was working the night shift at the local lumberyard.

Out of such a disloyal and dysfunctional environment, John's "will" had been inhibited by fear, causing a lack of freedom to trust anyone. This same restraint caused Kathleen to shut herself in and everyone else out, except for John. However, their souls would begin to secretly cry out for freedom from the fear, which held them both captive.

How does this contagious sense of fear manifest itself in the lives of people like John and Kathleen? It is one of satan's tactics. Fear is a dreadful emotion, which taunts the mind and disables the will from operating in liberty and in accordance with the principles of God. When we

## Taking Out The Trash

are not seeking and responding accordingly to the instructions given in the Word of God, we are unaware of the power and the authority that we have to resist the devil.

The Bible tells us that if we submit to God, resist the devil then he has to flee. The key to the power and the authority is the submission. The refusal to submit to God's word is the refusal to the power and authority over the enemy. Acts of rebellion gives place for a stronghold of fear, which dominates the area of the mind.

Now, the soul (mind, will and emotions) becomes out of order with the promises of God and the Spirit of God. The spirit of fear takes total control over an individual's mind, meanwhile taking captive the individual's will with an emotion of dreadfulness.

As the old cliche goes, "There is no rest for the weary." Kathleen's co-dependency has led her through life with no peace. The Bible says that we are to pursue peace. The soul must have order and connection, in order to be at rest. The peace of God does not abide in Kathleen's life because she has chosen not to pursue it. The peace comes when we are in pursuit of the peace-giver. And there must be a connection made to the One who is Peace.

## Fell By The Wayside

**The soul (mind, will and emotions) of a man must be in harmony with the spirit of a man who seeks to be in harmony with the Spirit of God. Where this threefold harmony exists, there is peace.**

The soul can be at rest when it is connected to the spirit of a man, then his spirit can receive peace from the Spirit of God.

The Bible tells us that where the Spirit of the Lord is we can find liberty. Here is where we can find the freedom that we seek from fear and turmoil. Fear restricts the flow of peace and controls one's actions and ability to use sound judgement.

Fear has one main objective for those who come face to face with it? It causes one to have dread or apprehension. This emotion of alarm is caused by the expectation of danger or failure. **The mind, the will and the emotions can become the hostages of fear. The dread in the mind causes an emotion of alarm, which apprehends the will from responding freely.** These are some of the crippling effects of the bondage of fear.

Fear offers no peace and no rest but God offers love, peace and a sound mind. Freedom insists that we do not have to accept anything that is contrary to the Word of God.

# Taking Out The Trash

> *(2 Timothy 1:7) "For God has not given us a spirit of fear, but of power and of love and of a sound mind."*

As born-again Christians, God has given us a spirit of power, love and a sound mind. When we accept Jesus Christ as personal Savior, who promises to us an abundant life, the Holy Spirit immediately comes and begins to free us from the bondage that keeps us bound. We become new creations because all old things have passed away and all things have become new.

The Holy Spirit comes to place a hedge of protection around us from the enemy. The attacks will come, but not prevail over the Word of God and its promises.

> *(Psalm 27:1,2) "The Lord is my light and my salvation; Whom shall I fear? The Lord is the strength of my life; Of whom shall I be afraid? When the wicked came against me To eat up my flesh, My enemies and foes, They stumbled and fell."*

In Kathleen's relationship with John, there was certainly evidence of a lack of peace, as well as trust.

**Many relationships fail, because they lack this one key ingredient. Trust in a relationship is as**

## Fell By The Wayside

important as the yeast in a loaf of bread. One must have the other, lest it falls and cease to rise.

How stable is a house framed together with commitment, but built on a foundation of distrust and fear? **The foundation must first be established with truth.** Once the foundation is laid with truth, then you must build up the trust.

Learning to trust is a process. The process begins with the admission of truth about one's self. Recognizing the need for a Savior allows the Truth to come to men, like John, whose souls have been bruised and whose spirits have been broken.

Salvation cleanses the heart through forgiveness. Jesus will wash away the fragments of the past. He repairs the broken spirit, which then prepares the broken heart to receive the promises of God. When you can receive this truth, the healing process can begin.

Jesus will become the father John never knew and even the father, whom you may have never known. Restoration begins with a simple prayer of repentance. God can and will extend his tender mercies and grace. He will cleanse your heart by *taking out the trash* that weighs so heavily.

## Taking Out The Trash

Maybe this day, you (John) could say to the Lord:

> *"Have mercy upon me, O God, according to Your steadfast love; according to the multitude of Your tender mercy and loving-kindness blot out my transgressions. Wash me thoroughly [and repeatedly] from my iniquity and guilt and cleanse me and make me wholly pure from my sin! For I am conscious of my transgressions and I acknowledge them; my sin is ever before me." (Psalm 51:1-3) (AMP)*

We must start with the acknowledgement of sin and the need for a Savior. Repentance to God shows accountability with an apology.

> *"Against You, You only, have I sinned and done that which is evil in Your sight, so that You are justified in Your sentence and faultless in your judgement. Behold, I was brought forth in [a state of] iniquity; my mother was sinful who conceived me [and I too am sinful]. Behold, You desire truth in the inner being; make me therefore to know wisdom in my inmost heart." (Psalm 51:4-6) (AMP)*

We must let God know the desire for change and the longing for His presence.

> *"Purify me with hyssop, and I shall be clean [ceremonially]; wash me, and I shall [in reality]*

## Fell By The Wayside

*be whiter than snow. Make me to hear joy and gladness and be satisfied; let the bones which You have broken rejoice. Hide Your face from my sins and blot out all my guilt and iniquities. Create in me a clean heart, O God, and renew a right, persevering, and steadfast spirit within me. Cast me not away from Your presence and take not Your Holy Spirit from me. Restore to me the joy of Your Salvation and uphold me with a willing spirit." (Psalm 51:7-12) (AMP) Amen.*

What an opportunity to call upon the name of the Lord and become a new creation in Christ. *"Therefore, if anyone is in Christ, he is a new creation; old things have passed away; behold, all things have become new." (2 Cor. 5:17)* Allowing God to begin the process of taking out the trash transforms the old man or woman into whom God has predestined us to become.

For many of us there is a fork in the road to our destiny. What determines our choice of path?

**There are two pathways set before us, both of which are designated as "Reflection" because they both appear to be the same.**

What is our mostly likely choice? We often choose the road that reflects who we think we are rather than the road

## Taking Out The Trash

which reflects who Jesus Christ says that we are. The instinct is to gravitate towards that which is familiar.

The problem exists when familiarity breeds deception. What has become familiar and comfortable to us is not always what is true to us. So, how can we recognize and choose the road to true destiny and freedom?

The answer requires the knowledge of truth, because the Word of God says to know the truth shall make us free. We can become free to make sound and wise decisions.

What does it mean to know truth? If you will for a moment, imagine yourself locked inside of a cage. You are standing at the entrance of the cage, facing forward and fiercely embracing the bars. You look down and see a key lying on the ground within your reach. But for the sake of this analogy, you do not know or recognize what the key is and therefore, do not know the purpose for which it is intended. So you just stand glaring at it, while becoming baffled by its existence. The tragedy is that you remain in bondage.

On the other hand, if you knew the truth about the key and it's representation, you would reach for it, pick it up and use it for the purpose in which it is intended. The

# Fell By The Wayside

purpose of the key is to unlock the cage and make you free.

By not knowing the truth (what the key is and its purpose), you remain in bondage behind the bars. So, the truth will not make you free, until you recognize it, as truth. The key will only make you free, when you know its representation and its purpose. The purpose is to unlock the doorway to your freedom.

The key symbolizes Jesus Christ. But we must first recognize Him as Truth. You can be set free by reaching out to Jesus and grabbing a hold of your freedom. The liberation comes through making the connection to the one who is Truth.

*"Jesus said to him, "I am the way, the truth, and the life. No one comes to the Father except through Me".." (John 14:6)* Jesus is saying that He is the way to the truth in life. He is the way to an abundant life of freedom. If your situation seems dark and without a means to an end, Jesus is the light to your pathway, the pathway to your freedom. Reach out to Jesus, who is the key, and unlock the cage that has you so tightly bound. Jesus said to his disciples in John 8:32, *"And you shall know the truth, and the truth shall make you free."*

## Taking Out The Trash

The Spirit of God offers freedom to all of those who seek to know Him. We must know Him as the liberator. What is the meaning of "where the spirit of the Lord is there is freedom"? It means that where His spirit is connected to our spirits and to our souls, there is liberty! The soul has to be plugged in to the liberator! Without the connection, our souls cannot receive the liberation through the Spirit. The power of liberation flows from the source but we must plug into the source, in order to receive the power.

For example, there is usually a consistent flow of power within the electrical outlets in a house. So, we know that the power is present in that house to provide energy. Therefore, it is always accessible, but does not always provide light or energy, until it has been plugged into. So when the Spirit of the Lord is present in the house, the only ones who will receive light or liberty are the ones who are plugged in or connected!

Liberation does not come without a price. We must diligently seek to know the Truth.

**The knowledge of truth is liberating but the wisdom gained from truth is continuous freedom!**

It is one thing to be set free but there is always a cost to remain free.

## Fell By The Wayside

For Kathleen, freedom didn't last very long. A short while after, there came Bobby, who was seemingly nice and considerate. But along with Bobby, came a few bad habits. At this point, Bobby would be what we would consider an occasional user. Kathleen knew this, but thought he only smoked every once and a while. So, like many of us, she dismissed the red flag that was fiercely waving in front of her face.

How often do we dismiss warning signs in the beginning of relationships, simply because we think this could be the right one or that we can change him or her? Only to our surprise, before we can change them, they change us. We step outside of our established boundaries and begin to settle. The deception is that things will get better in time.

A year and a half into their relationship, things worsened. Bobby's occasional use became an obsessive, habitual, and costly habit. Once again, Kathleen found herself in captivity, bound by fear. Frantically, she began searching and turning the house inside and out. She kept desperately looking for her bracelet, not wanting to accept the fact that Bobby had pawned it.

The emeralds and diamonds now stood for about thirty seconds of pleasure coming from the end of a crack pipe.

# Taking Out The Trash

Eventually, other items began to disappear, one by one. Because of her nature as a co-dependent and not wanting to accuse Bobby directly, Kathleen began making excuses for his behavior. Except now, the bill collectors were no longer accepting anymore excuses as payment.

Kathleen continued to press in her own tracks of co-dependency by making excuses for Bobby's actions. Honestly believing that some day Bobby would change, she thought, "I will get a second job to cover his end, then no one will have to know."

Meanwhile Bobby was continuously trying to discover himself by using the credit card, which had been co-signed by Kathleen. Kathleen saw herself in another hopeless situation. For her, matters got even worse, Bobby decided that he wanted out.

Bobby believed he would feel more at home in his very own house, preferably the crack house.

This picture is played over and over daily in many lives. Somehow the life of Kathleen becomes absorbed even by Bobby's co-dependency. She allowed the needs and desires of Bobby to control her life. She enabled him by making excuses for his poor actions and choices. Co-dependents have a compulsive need to be responsible for the actions

## Fell By The Wayside

of others. This kind of lifestyle is unhealthy and unsafe for both Kathleen and Bobby.

The real tragedy in this kind of situation is double dependency. While Kathleen is dependent on Bobby, he is dependent on substances and there is no true dependency on God. If you are currently in a situation like Kathleen or Bobby, I encourage you to get out immediately and seek outside help from a relative, friend, local church or organization. You can start by asking God for direction in this area. Isaiah 28:29 reads, *"This also comes from the LORD of hosts, who is wonderful in counsel and excellent in guidance."* You can begin to trust God to direct your path!

> *(Proverbs 3:5,6) "Trust in the LORD with all your heart, And lean not on your own understanding; In all your ways acknowledge Him, And He shall direct your paths."*

In all your ways acknowledge Him, even for the way out because Jesus is the way, truth and the life. He is the way to truth about your life and in your life.

We must become dependent on Jesus Christ and not on some false sense of security. While Kathleen's co-dependency is with people, Bobby's co-dependency derives

## Taking Out The Trash

from substance abuse. Co-dependency is an unhealthy and destructive addiction.

An addicted person has a compulsive need to surrender himself or herself habitually or obsessively to something or someone. This is the kind of trash that clutters our temple. This evil disease of substance abuse has come to destroy many lives but Jesus Christ has come so that we may have life and have it more abundantly.

If you are experiencing similar circumstances, allow Jesus Christ to take out the trash, so that you can present your body as a living sacrifice to Him. Which is holy and acceptable to God. This is your reasonable service and spiritual worship unto Him. Allow Jesus to take out the trash and fill your taste with His presence.

> *(Psalm 34:8-10) "Oh, taste and see that the Lord is good; Blessed is the man who trusts in Him! Oh, fear the Lord, you His saints! There is no want to those who fear Him. The young lions lack and suffer hunger; But those who seek the Lord shall not lack any good thing."*

Remember all old things have passed away and all things have become new for those who are in Jesus Christ. Deliverance comes through healing. Both Bobby and Kathleen must be healed of their past and their history of

## Fell By The Wayside

co-dependencies. Otherwise, they are destined to repeat them.

**Without a release of the past, it will graciously step into your future.**

With deliverance, there must also come a release of some people and/or things which hinder us from moving forward into a life style of independency, but not independent of Jesus Christ. Jesus Christ must be first and foremost the source from which we draw to sustain life. Jesus is the source and the supplier of whatever is or seems to be lacking in life. So if you hunger and thirst for anything, first taste and see that the Lord is good.

Maybe you are feeling trapped by this past that seems to overwhelm you with a sense of defeat? Maybe your heart has been broken time and time again? Jesus wants you to be encouraged by acknowledging Him who has all power. The power to create heaven and earth, to change night into day, to create woman from man, and undoubtedly to heal all who call on His name.

> *(Psalm 147:3) "He heals the brokenhearted*
> *And binds up their wounds."*

Have you been wounded? Jesus is the physician and the

## Taking Out The Trash

remedy. If you feel bound by your circumstances, Jesus can give you freedom. *"Now the Lord is the Spirit; and where the Spirit of the Lord is, there is liberty." (2 Cor. 3:17)* Now, all you have to do is get connected to the liberator.

> *(Luke 4:18) "The spirit of the LORD is upon Me, because He has anointed Me to preach the gospel to the poor. He has sent Me to heal the brokenhearted, to preach deliverance to the captives and recovery of sight to the blind, to set at liberty those who are oppressed."*

As you read and receive this Word into your heart, the healing process begins. The Spirit of the Lord is upon you, the brokenhearted, to be healed; and you, the captive, to be set free. Then you, who are bound, shall know the Truth and the Truth shall make you free.

Only you can open up the door and allow Jesus Christ to come in and take out the trash.

The enemy's purpose is to keep us stressed and confused with uncertainty. We all are faced with the trials and temptations in this life. Jesus' response to the turmoil of this world is that persecutions will come in this world but He has overcome the world. Many have been robbed of God's free gift, the gift of salvation. It is imperative that

## Fell By The Wayside

we understand the power of the Word and its importance in order to receive the promised gift of freedom and eternal life.

In the parable of the sower, the seeds (Word) that fell by the wayside represent the ones who hear the Word but the devil comes immediately and takes by force the Word out of their hearts, so that they cannot believe and receive salvation. Salvation not only gives eternal life but also gives us access to the healing and the deliverance from the hurts in this life.

Like Kathleen and Bobby, we must be saved from our sins. This means we must be saved from ourselves. Sin is conceived when we are drawn away from God unto our very own selfish pleasures. Satan offers us temporal things like sex, money and drugs. He makes promises that will only bring destruction.

Why do you think satan comes to take away by force the message of life from our hearts? The Bible says, *"Blessed is the man who endures temptation; for when he has been proved, he will receive the crown of life which the Lord has promised to those who love Him." (James 1:12)*

The word *force* indicates that some resistance occurs. The struggle exists because the (carnal man) flesh is enmity

# Taking Out The Trash

against the Spirit of God. This war is confirmed in the book of Romans. When the Word is heard, the temptation of sin immediately forces its way in and begins to try and dictate the course of our lives!

The blessings come once we have endured the temptation and have been proven. "Proven" is the past tense of the verb - prove. Which means to determine the quality of someone or something by testing. It establishes truth or validity through the presentation of argument or evidence.

The presentation of argument or evidence is the message of life that is presented. Once the Word is presented, heard and established as truth or validated, then the crown of life is received.

The Bible warns that satan goes all over the earth seeking someone to devour, because he wants to destroy you and God's divine will for your life.

But once salvation is received, life is received and the enemy cannot destroy you. That's why, he comes immediately to take the Word away from your heart, lest you believe and the Word becomes validated and you are proven to be righteous. Salvation acknowledges the very presence of a Savior!

## Fell By The Wayside

*(Romans 8:10) "And if Christ is in you, the body is dead because of sin, but the Spirit is life because of righteousness."*

Where does the common ground exist for most of us? It is the battle between the temporal and the eternal. Take Kathleen who does go to church about twice a month and really likes the music. However, she is not so sure about her salvation but acknowledges that she is a good person.

Going to church is good and can be convenient for our temporal lives. Yet we never receive salvation which is good for our eternal lives.

Unfortunately, we sometimes take part of the truth and use it for our own selfish appeasement. Sometimes the complete truth does not taste good to us but it is always good for us. The taste is never good to our flesh. But Jesus warns us that no flesh shall glory in His presence. However, satan does glory in the flesh. Only when we submit to the Word of God, can we gain victory over the enemy who brings destruction through our very own selfish and lustful pleasures. Destruction begins with self and ends with self.

Those who seek to satisfy their own selfish desires cannot please God. The Bible says that the carnal mind (flesh) is

## Taking Out The Trash

enmity against God. Therefore, a war exists between the spirit and the carnal nature of man. The truth is that we are fleshly beings who physically see and feel the adversities which come against us, but the weapons used to war against the adversary are not seen or felt in the natural. 2 Corinthians 10: 3,4 states, *"For though we walk in the flesh, we do not war according to the flesh. For the weapons of our warfare are not carnal but mighty in God for pulling down strongholds."*

This means although we live in the world, we do not fight from worldly perspectives. The weapons we use to fight with are not the world's weapons but the powerful weapons of God.

The scriptures go on to say, *"casting down arguments and every high thing that exalts itself against the knowledge of God, bringing every thought into captivity to the obedience of Christ." (2 Cor. 10:5)*

It is the Word of God that pulls down everything that rises up or exalts itself against the knowledge of Jesus Christ. The pulling down of strongholds begins in the mind. The Sword of the Spirit must bring every thought that tries to bring satisfaction to the flesh, under submission. The Sword of the Spirit that we use to fight off the enemy's attacks is the powerful Word of God.

## Fell By The Wayside

So, I challenge you to put on the entire armor that God gives to empower us to stand up against the wiles (methods) of the devil and his deceitful tricks. God instructs us as His children how to prepare ourselves for the daily battle against satan's evil attacks in Ephesians.

> *"Finally, let the mighty strength of the Lord make you strong. Put on all the armor that God gives, so you can defend yourself against the devil's tricks. We are not fighting against humans. We are fighting against forces and authorities and against rulers of darkness and powers in the spiritual world.*
> *So put on all the armor that God gives. Then when that evil day comes, you will be able to defend yourself. And when the battle is over, you will still be standing firm. Be ready! Let the truth be like a belt around your waist, and let God's justice protect you like armor. Your desire to tell the good news about peace should be like shoes on your feet. Let your faith be like a shield, and you will be able to stop all the flaming arrows of the evil one. Let God's saving power be like a helmet, and for a sword use God's message that comes from the Spirit.*
> *Never stop praying, especially for others. Always pray by the power of the Spirit. Stay alert and keep praying for God's people."(Eph. 6:10-18) (CEV)*

## Taking Out The Trash

We can prepare for victory by putting on the whole armor which is truth, righteousness, peace, salvation, faith and our sword, which is the Word of God. Godly wisdom teaches that no wise man would go to war without first counting up the cost of victory.

This is a moment of truth for all who will receive it. Right now, you can accept Jesus Christ as your personal Savior. He is the one whom you have been searching for. The Holy Spirit can teach you to guard your heart from the devices of the enemy. I John 5:18 states, *"We know that whoever is born of God does not sin; but he who has been born of God keeps himself, and the wicked one does not touch him."* This is Jesus' promise of protection when we come to know Him as the true God. So, receive your protection by confessing that Jesus is Lord and accepting Him as your personal Savior. There is no reason to remain among the lost sheepfold that goes unprotected. I John 5:19 says, *"We know that we are of God, and the whole world lies under the sway of the wicked one."* Our only assurance of safety is that our Father, who saves us from out of this world, will also protect us in this world.

Jesus, who is the good shepherd, will watch over you and cover you in His anointing. He will go before you in your daily walk. The Good Shepherd goes before His sheep and

# Fell By The Wayside

His sheep follows behind Him for they know His voice and will not follow another.

> *(John 10:14-16) "I am the good shepherd; and I know My sheep, and am known by My own. "As the Father knows Me, even so I know the Father; and I lay down My life for the sheep. "And other sheep I have which are not of this fold; them also I must bring, and they will hear My voice; and there will be one flock and one shepherd."*

At this very moment, the voice of the "Good Shepherd" is whispering to you to follow after Him and He will keep you and protect you.

# Taking Out The Trash

## Food For Thought

- *The seeds that Fell By The Wayside are those who hear but the devil comes immediately to take the Word away from their hearts.*

- *Co-dependents, who are addicted to people, feel that there has to be someone or a significant other in their lives at all times.*

- *Co-dependents often lose sight of their own personal feelings and needs.*

- *Fear is a dreadful emotion, which taunts the mind and disables the will from operating in freedom.*

- *The refusal to submit to God's word is the refusal to the power and authority over the enemy.*

- *Peace comes when we are in pursuit of the Peace-Giver.*

- *Trust in a relationship is as important as the yeast in a loaf of bread.*

- *We often choose the road that reflects who we think we are rather than the road which reflect who Jesus Christ says that we are.*

- *What has become familiar and comfortable to us is not always what is true to us.*

## Fell By The Wayside

- *The knowledge of truth is liberating but the wisdom gained from truth is continuous freedom!*

- *Without a release of the past, it will graciously step into your future.*

- *Godly wisdom teaches that no wise man would go to war without first counting up the cost of victory.*

- *Once the Word is presented, heard and established as truth or validated, then the crown of life is received.*

# Taking Out The Trash

# 6
# Warning!!! Beware Of Thorns

§

Single people may sometimes feel like second-class citizens in life and especially in the church where much of the focus and activity is centered on the family unit.

A family is traditionally thought of as a unit, which consists of a mother, father and a child or children. Many singles, especially single parents, are wondering where they fit into this mold. Being single can sometimes bring about great frustration and confusion. It oftentimes causes thorns that can linger and pierce the very depths of our souls.

# Taking Out The Trash

Many questions are often raised concerning these issues. What does God require of me as a single person? How am I to conduct myself as a single Christian? What are the rules governing single Christianity, particularly in dating?

These, among many other unanswered questions, have led to many singles living one of the most unpleasing lifestyles. God explicitly forbids this lifestyle among singles and especially Christians. This is a lifestyle that has been cluttered with the trash of fornication.

Fornication is having sexual relations outside the confines of marriage. Colossians 3: 5,6 states, *"Therefore put to death your members which are on the earth: fornication, uncleanness, passion, evil desire, and covetousness, which is idolatry. Because of these things the wrath of God is coming upon the sons of disobedience."*

This is a warning as to the severity of disobedience to God's word concerning sexual immorality or fornication. It is an issue that we must address and there is no greater time than now.

Loneliness is a big concern for singles. We know fornication is wrong but somehow we can always justify our actions. We seem to find the right excuse at the right

## Warning!!! Beware Of Thorns

time, besides we are human, and of course, the Lord will forgive us because He understands.

Do these words, which are often used as wrongful justification, ring a bell? For single women and men there are no excuses or justifications. Fornication is not God's will for us. God's desire is for His children to live holy lives by walking in the ways of the Lord.

When we become born-again Christians, a relationship or covenant is established between Jesus Christ and us. Our bodies and our spirits now belong to the Lord. They no longer belong to us. The body is a temple of the Holy Spirit. We were bought for a price with the blood of Jesus Christ. He gave His life for us. As His sons and daughters, the Holy Spirit now dwells within us. Fornication dishonors the body and the Holy Spirit who is within.

When we have the knowledge of truth, the truth will make us free. The body is a holy temple in which the Holy Spirit dwells. Wherever we go, the Holy Spirit goes. Whatever we do with our bodies, the Spirit who is within us is there along with us. So when the flesh desires to commit sexual immoral acts or fornication, remember the Holy Spirit.

When truth comes to enlighten us, it is often accompanied by a sense of uneasiness or with an uncomfortable feeling.

# Taking Out The Trash

And it should. We should not grieve, hurt or cause sorrow to the Holy Spirit.

Ephesians 4:30 solicits our respect for Him by saying, *"And do not grieve the Holy Spirit of God, by whom you were sealed for the day of redemption."* Flee from sexual immorality!

> *(1 Corinthians 6:18-20) "Flee sexual immorality. Every sin that a man does is outside the body, but he who commits sexual immorality sins against his own body. Or do you not know that your body is the temple of the Holy Spirit who is in you, whom you have from God, and you are not your own? For you were bought at a price; therefore glorify God in your body and in your spirit, which are God's."*

Has fornication become a thorn in your life? The warning is to beware of thorns. Make your body holy and acceptable to God by *taking out the trash*. Like Paul, the Apostle, we must buffet (force) our bodies to submit to the spiritual authority of the Holy Spirit.

Many of us learn by example. We watch how the world operates, as it lusts after the riches that seem to make it turn. We watch our parents rushing here and there, many times not seeming to have the time for anything, even us.

## Warning!!! Beware Of Thorns

We look for role models when our parents should have been our greatest role models.

Most parents set good patterns and give good instructions to their children. They want to build good character in their children and teach them to become responsible adults. But there is the parent who always says, to the already confused child, "Do as I say, not as I do!"

This statement would even sound confusing to an adult, coming from someone who he or she admires and trusts.

What patterns have been set in motion by your parents? Children watch and retain their parent's behavior. They watch how their parents function and cope with life situations on a day-to-day basis. They watch how their parents interact with others, particularly people of the opposite sex.

One of the most important learned behaviors in a child's life is the interaction between mom and dad. If a circumstance exists where either the mother or father is absent, interaction with whomever operating in the role of counterpart will be looked upon as the example.

The Bible gives us sound wisdom about molding children into good, moral and responsible adults.

# Taking Out The Trash

*"Train up a child in the way he should go, And when he is old he will not depart from it." (Prov. 22:6)*

Unfortunately no one told Jade's mother how and where to get some of this sound wisdom. As a child of a single parent, Jade watched her mom's leisure lifestyle.

On Thursday night, Tom would come by and he would always bring a gift for Jade. She really looked forward to Friday night because Mr. Ed would come with a new toy to add to her collection.

Saturday had somewhat of a different twist, because Jade was left with the neighbors while her mom and the preacher went away for the afternoon.

This was okay with Jade because Mr. Preacher always promised to bring her something pretty. Jade didn't really understand what was going on but somehow she could relate to the pattern of her mother's behavior.

What Jade could relate to was that for every new and different date which mom entertained, came a new and different toy.

Unfortunately as an adult, Jade still practices this same irrational, unhealthy, but learned behavior. She thought,

## Warning!!! Beware Of Thorns

"A different guy, a different gift." But now, there is a trade-off to receiving such wonderful things. She has to give something in return for her gifts, her body. Unconsciously, Jade continued in her mother's promiscuous ways.

Jade became sexually active at very young age. She started to search for the missing pieces in her life. When she was four, Jade's father walked out on her and her mother. She often wondered what he was like and why he left them. Maybe he left for the same reasons Michael left her.

Jade was divorced from Michael only after two-and-a-half years of marriage. The lies and deceit destroyed the marriage and led to adultery. However, Jade rejoiced over the one good thing that came out of such a bad relationship. Damion is now seven and looks so much like his father.

Because of Jade's difficulty making ends meet after the divorce, he went to live with his grandmother.

Since Damion only comes over to visit every other weekend, Jade now has more time to spend with Leon. She knew the relationship was headed in the right direction, when she finally convinced Leon to go along to church. This seemed a little bit ironic coming from someone who had been constantly invited to church by friends and always responded by saying, "If it's the Lord's will, I'll be there."

Somehow, in Jade's mind, she had convinced herself that it was ok, just as long as she went to church every once and a while. Besides, now she has a great job, a nice place to live and a new car, so she must be living right.

It's funny how deception can rule a person's life and give reason to justify his or her actions. Leon was another blessing from God because he was the man Jade had been praying for. She knew God would soon send her the right one.

Jade, like many who live deceptive lives; believes that these possessions are truly blessings coming from God. Jade believes in her heart that she is truly fulfilling the will of God. Carnal (worldly, fleshly or temporal) minds think what is referred to as the "American Dream" of wealth and riches, once achieved, results from right standing with God. This assumption is based only on their possessions.

So we continue to give thanks to God by giving Him just a little bit of our time and money. Jade's thanks is to go to

## Warning!!! Beware Of Thorns

church every once and a while to show her gratitude.

Can we possibly go through life with the belief that obtaining material gains is the answer to one of the most profound questions ever asked by God himself?

Jesus once asked his disciples a very important question, "Who do you say I am?"

What the world does not recognize is that God is no fool. He is the Holy and all-wise God who operates on the principle of sowing and reaping. If one plants in the field of his natural desires (fleshly things), from it he will gather a harvest of death and curses. If one sows in the field of the Spirit, he will gather a harvest of eternal life and blessings. Things do not impress our God, because He created all things.

The possessions can become our idol, which becomes our god. This deception creates a false sense of assurance about what a relationship is with Jesus Christ. What might your response be to the question? Would it be that same response the world would give?

*(Galatians 6:7,8) "Do not be deceived, God is not mocked; for whatever a man sows, that he will*

## Taking Out The Trash

*also reap. For he who sows to his flesh will of the flesh reap corruption, but he who sows to the Spirit will of the Spirit reap everlasting life."*

The deception lies in the fulfillment of self. Selfishness breeds corruption and corruption leads to death. Jade's self-gratification led her into self-indulgence. Self-indulgence is to overly indulge in one's own appetites and fleshly desires.

From a very young age, Jade was accustomed to getting things. In return for such lavish gifts, there was a trade-off, which opened avenues for destruction. For a long time, Jade could not figure out what was going on inside of her body and mind. She wondered why her marriage didn't last. There had to be a reason why her ex-husband could not satisfy her.

By becoming sexually active at a young age, Jade created a great appetite for sex and there was a constant hunger to be satisfied, a hunger that her husband alone could not fulfill. So, Jade's answer to the problem was to find her husband some help.

What could be the root cause of Jade's sexual perverseness? Why did she choose this path for her life?

## Warning!!! Beware Of Thorns

Or did she choose this path? Our lives are structured by our choices. Some choices are good and some are bad. With every choice comes the by-product of consequences. Our lives reflect the consequences of those choices and some of our parents' choices.

Our parents made a decision to have sex, which produced a seed that produced a child. Further decisions were made about how to raise up the child. Through this process came Jade's life experiences which influenced her choices and her behaviors.

Jade is her parent's seed and the product of some of her mother's choices. A seed will produce after its own kind when it is watered and nurtured. Jade's mother chose to water her seed with sexual perversion. The perverted magazines that Jade found set the tone and subjected them to a lifestyle of perverseness. And the enemy used this opportunity to twist Jade's sexuality.

*Proverbs 26:2 says, "Like a flitting sparrow, like a flying swallow, So a curse without a cause shall not alight."* There is always a cause for a curse and it has many effects. The cause gives the enemy the legal right to bring destruction in a person's life. Pornography opens the door for satan to destroy families, and individual lives. The result is an indulgence in sexual sins that are passed from generation to generation. The consequences can affect many people without their knowledge.

What Jade did not know was that soul ties or covenants were formed with all the men she had slept with. Jade had become one with all of her sexual partners. There were now many appetites to be satisfied in one body, Jade's body. Sexual intimacy between two people creates a bonding of the bodies and of the souls. The Bible gives us great detail in 1 Corinthians 6:16, which states: *"Or do you not know that he who is joined to a harlot is one body with her? For "The two," He says, "shall become one flesh."*

A soul tie is a bond between two people's souls, which consist of their minds, wills and emotions.

The bond is formed through an agreement by decision in the (mind), to (will) to give of one's feelings or sensibilities (emotions) to another.

Ungodly soul ties can be formed through fornication or sexual relations and are most often based on lust. The desire is to satisfy a physical appetite. Each time sexual intimacy takes place outside the confines of marriage; the individuals involved lose a part of their soul. They

## Warning!!! Beware Of Thorns

individually will to the other, a part of his or her being. As their bodies are joined, so are their souls and they become one. This is a covenant that God intended for the bonding of a husband and wife. A husband shall leave his mother and father and become one with his wife.

As a result of fornication, each individual goes his or her separate way, only to take a part of the other person's soul with him or her. The compounding effect is that you lose a part of your soul and gain a part of another's soul.

The real tragedy takes place once you are married. You now have nothing or only part of yourself to give to your spouse.

Then, there is an expectation of your spouse to satisfy a part of you that does not truly belong to you. Instead, he or she is trying to fulfill a part of your soul, which actually belongs to another whom he or she has no idea about. Therefore, that which belongs to another has to be released by you. Also, to become whole in body, soul and spirit, one must reclaim that which was taken from him or her by another.

How can we love the Lord, thy God with all our heart, mind and soul when parts of our souls are now with Fred,

# Taking Out The Trash

Bobby and James or with Stacey and Marie? Surely, you can get the point. Soul ties are binding covenants and must be broken by the renouncing of the fragmented pieces and a reclaiming of wholeness through the Word of God. This severs the ties and frees the soul.

Proverbs 4:7 says, *"Wisdom is the principal thing; Therefore get wisdom. And in all your getting, get understanding."* We cannot use wisdom until we understand the cause and the effect. Sexual sins and sexual perversions establish soul ties. Both are the result of a curse from the enemy. The enemy understands that he must have a cause or a legal right to kill, steal and destroy. He has no legal right without an open door which to enter in. We have to recognize the cause and renounce the curse. The wisdom is shutting the door and keeping it shut. This is essential for everyone who desires to be free of sexual immoralities and to live a victorious life in Jesus Christ.

Jade lived a somewhat normal life by day but struggled with a great appetite for sex. It was so great that she could not be committed to one relationship "Nor" be committed to God. Unfortunately, her selfishness and discontentment caused hurt for others. The men, who were in Jade's life, were as equally victims.

## Warning!!! Beware Of Thorns

It would be wonderful, if behind every good man, there was truly a good woman. Randy had the right idea but the wrong woman. He was desperately looking for the right woman but in the wrong places. Randy had begun to think that his biological clock was rapidly ticking away. Even though Randy had children from previous marriages, he desired a family. He had hoped to find a wife and a mother for his children.

As a result of two failed marriages, Randy felt an overwhelming sense of rejection. This stronghold made Randy feel that no woman would want a man who already had several children. Randy was convinced that there must be something wrong with him because he was not able to maintain a lasting and meaningful relationship. He was unable to recognize that there was limited space in his life because he was cohabitating with this spirit of fear of failure.

A stronghold had developed through Randy's feelings of rejection. He lived with a sense of defeat and hopelessness. Randy could not live up to the standards which he thought were necessary to please the women in his life, simply because the standards he was trying to live up to were not real or valid indicators of his true ability. The

# Taking Out The Trash

strongholds or false illusions were created in Randy's mind and perceived by him to be valid reasons for being rejected by women. The spirit of rejection reinforced the stronghold of fear.

This False Evidence Appearing Real (FEAR) was being used by the enemy to hold Randy's mind captive. There was a fear of never finding the right person, which caused Randy to become overly anxious.

The stronghold of fear occupied and dominated Randy's mind and held him captive with the dread of failure. A stronghold can become a fortified area in a person's life through fear, doubt, rejection, anger, bitterness, and unforgiveness.

Fortunately, Randy became recommitted to Jesus Christ and was excited about reuniting with his Father. Still, there was one thing missing. Randy thought, "If I could just change Jade, she would be the perfect wife and mother."

He even tried to encourage her change by giving her a Bible. Having fallen into the trap of trying to change someone, Randy continued in the relationship, despite his many failed attempts.

## Warning!!! Beware Of Thorns

Jade knew the kind of commitment Randy was looking for, but she had another agenda. Jade was only concerned with the material things and her selfish ends.

While trying to reinforce his relationship with Jesus Christ, Randy vowed to celibacy until he was married and he continued to fight the good fight of faith.

Jade thought, "Well, he is a man and he won't last long." So, she made great efforts to lure him away from his belief. Jade was very clear about what she wanted and needed.

Randy was sure they were making some progress because Jade was now going to church with him on a regular basis. Randy was impressed and remained hopeful. This was a step in the right direction but Jade would never attend church without him. Even his attempts to get her to pray with him were unsuccessful.

Could this be red flag number two or number twenty-two? But who's counting?

The warning is to be aware of thorns. Thorns will hinder our growth and our progress. Sometimes what seems good and looks good is not always good for us.

# Taking Out The Trash

How many times have we gotten the answer needed for that other question? The question is can this be the one? Warning signs come to us in many forms. It may be in the form of a response to a question or a reaction to a certain situation. It can be uneasiness in the innermost being which prompts us to wait a moment before proceeding. We can tell a lot about a person through his or her conversation and even more so by his or her actions or reactions. We all should have an idea of the qualities that we desire in another and then set in place boundaries to keep us positioned and focused.

When we get outside of our set limits or someone crosses over those limits, this is a warning not to proceed. This is a red flag, which means to stop and examine the situation, listen and check yourself.

Because Randy wanted so much for this to be the right person, he was blinded by his own selfish gains. Randy's life is a reflection of the Biblical story of Samson, who was a man of great destiny but one who lost his focus.

The book of Judges tells of the birth of Samson who was born to a woman who was once barren. But after the angel of the Lord appeared to her, He announced her conception of a son and gave her specific instructions. The child would be born a Nazirite to God from the womb.

## Warning!!! Beware Of Thorns

Later born under the Nazirite vow, Samson would have to live a life of consecration and devotion to the Lord. And as a condition of the Nazirite vow, no razor was to ever touch Samson's head.

The Lord's purpose for Samson was to deliver the children of Israel out of the hands of the Philistines who were always at war with the Israelites. Because the Israelites had done evil and disobeyed the Lord, He gave them over to the hands of the Philistines for forty years.

Samson would later develop a love-hate relationship with the Philistines. He becomes drawn to them by the attraction to one of the Philistines' daughters. Against his parents' wishes, Samson would make her his bride. Samson insisted on her as his choice, because she pleased him well. A short time later, Samson would experience one of his greatest trials. His Philistine wife would betray him.

During a time of regular feasting, the great Samson posed a riddle for the Philistines to solve. After three days, the Philistines were unable to resolve the riddle. So, they began to threaten Samson's wife. Out of fear, she pressed Samson for the answer and revealed it to the Philistine men. Her father concluded that she would be greatly hated by Samson and gave her to Samson's best man.

# Taking Out The Trash

Samson sought revenge and showed no mercy towards the Philistines. The Philistines retaliated by setting on fire Samson's bride and her father. In an act of vengeance, the Spirit of the Lord came upon Samson and he destroyed a thousand Philistines with the jawbone of a donkey.

Then Samson ventured to the city of Gaza where he met a harlot by the name of Delilah. Approached by the Philistine lords to find the source of Samson's strength, she pressed Samson daily until he told her all of his heart. After discovering the source of Samson's strength, the Philistine lords came to shave off the seven locks from Samson's head. Then Samson lost the source of his power and broke his Nazirite vow.

Like Samson, Randy had been drawn away from God by his very own lust and desire for women.

In the past Randy had experienced many relationships with many different women. Now, facing the law of sowing and reaping, Randy would meet his match with Jade.

His Delilah had come to conquer him. Jade's character seemed much like that of Delilah who pressured Samson daily in order to obtain knowledge on how to drain his great strength from him.

## Warning!!! Beware Of Thorns

What happened to Samson when he encountered Delilah? Notice that Delilah was not concerned with Samson's weaknesses, but rather (the source or cause of) Samson's strength.

Rather than focusing on his many possible weaknesses, Delilah went straight to the main source of strength. Once the source is cut off, many weaknesses become exposed because many channels or openings can flow from the main source.

Once the main source of power is shut off, all outlets become defective or of no use. Then the enemy can target our weaknesses.

In order for Delilah to gain total control, she had to first cut off Samson's source of power, his hair. Ironically, at the same point of Samson's strength, also lies his weakness.

Maybe Jesus had this in mind when he said, "His strength is made in our weakness."

Once Samson's source, the seven locks, was cut off, his weaknesses were exposed. Samson's hair was symbolic of his Nazirite vow of holy commitment to God.

# Taking Out The Trash

Samson was committed to holiness from his mother's womb. A covenant was established by God and with God. This covenant was also a sign of God's personal commitment and protection to Samson and his family.

The enemy's plan is to make our weakness become an exposé, the revealing of something discreditable or blameworthy. The Bible refers to satan as the "accuser of the brethren." He wants to expose you in order to discredit you. Because the blood of Jesus covers your weaknesses, once they are exposed there is no protection or covering. When you take away the source, who is Jesus, you take away the covering and your weaknesses become the evidence used by the enemy to accuse you.

The enemy wanted to use Randy's past lifestyle as evidence to expose his weaknesses. What is so wonderful is that the blood of Jesus dismisses the evidence when we remain in covenant with the *Source*.

Both Jade and Delilah came with a demonically-inspired plan to expose the weaknesses of their men. Jade's intentions were not to get her soul saved, but she was willing to go along for the ride, as long as necessary. Besides, Randy was making her task easier by stepping outside his boundaries. Jade knew it was only a matter of time before he would give in.

## Warning!!! Beware Of Thorns

Many late evening visits would play right into her hands. Randy thought this would be the perfect time to talk to her about some of his interests. Randy put himself in a position of compromise and this was confirmed when he heard a little voice softly whispering, "I got you now."

Jade was finally winning the battle but Randy wasn't going out without a fight.

Suddenly, a way of escape, the telephone rang. Randy began to recognize this familiar place of compromise. Jade was very strong willed about what she wanted, as is the adversary. If we can be persuaded to step beyond our set boundaries, we then step into a place of compromise or even surrender.

Men can be as vulnerable as women. Be it man or woman, when put into a compromising position, the opportunity arises to surrender to the carnal nature. Randy was on the right track in seeking the Lord but he lacked patience, not to mention, wisdom. If he had been patient and continued to faithfully trust God for his mate, then God would have been faithful to bring him someone who desired the same personal commitment to Jesus Christ. Remember what looks good, is not always good for us.

# Taking Out The Trash

The experiences told in these passages are designed to prompt you to consider your position of authority and stewardship. The authority comes from knowing who you are in Jesus Christ and what He expects of your stewardship over what He has entrusted to you. You must know that you have within, the Spirit of God who rules over your carnal (fleshly) nature. God has entrusted you as a steward over His body.

Your body does not belong to you. Jesus bought you for a price and your body is now a holy temple of God. Let us not compromise our position of promise. You can begin now by *Taking Out The Trash*.

Randy and Jade both lived the story of Samson whose vision was blinded as soon as he saw Delilah. Her beauty blinded Samson and he could not see the forest for the trees. The story tells how Samson's mother and father questioned Samson's judgement in his choice of a woman. Samson was so sure of his decision that he responded by saying that she was well-pleasing in his eyes.

In essence, he was saying that, "she looked good and I have got to have her." It's my choice and it's my life. What he was really saying in rebellion was that "I want what I want." Even, Samson was governed by rules as a Nazirite, so he had boundaries set in place by God.

# Warning!!! Beware Of Thorns

It is never a good idea to compromise your commitment to the Lord. Randy was able to endure because of his love for the Lord. The Bible says, "A man is blessed to endure temptation."

There is no temptation that comes to you beyond your power to overcome it and at the time of testing, God will give you the strength to endure and a way out.

*(1Corinthians 10: 12,13) "Therefore let him who thinks he stands take heed lest he fall. No temptation has overtaken you except such as is common to man; but God is faithful, who will not allow you to be tempted beyond what you are able, but with the temptation will also make the way of escape, that you may be able to bear it."*

When the temptation comes, the way of escape must be recognized and utilized. Unlike Samson who was unable to recognize his way of escape, he was tempted or enticed three times by Delilah before he revealed his heart to her. The Bible says that after she had pressed him persistently day after day with her words, Samson's soul was vexed to death. His soul became so weaken that he revealed the source of his power. Samson told Delilah that if his head were shaven, then all his strength would leave him. He would become weak and be like any other man.

# Taking Out The Trash

When Delilah had gained all that Samson knew, she called for the Philistines to come once more. They brought with them the money to exchange for the secrets to Samson's great strength.

While Samson was soothed to sleep upon Delilah's knees, a man came and shaved off the seven braids on Samson's head. Delilah began to torment Samson and his strength left him. Samson tried to fight off the attack of the Philistines but the Lord had departed from him.

There is a great lesson in Samson's trials. Samson paid a price for his disobedience and his selfish motives. He had broken the Nazirite vow (commitment) to God by stepping outside of his boundaries (covenant).

God called Samson even before he was in his mother's womb. God knew Samson's heart and He had a purpose for Samson's life. That purpose was to deliver Israel out of the hands of the Philistines. The Lord was creating a timely opportunity to destroy the Philistines. So he allowed Samson to meet Delilah. God knew beforehand that Samson would fall because of his disobedience, as with us. That is why God sent us a Savior who uses our situations by creating timely opportunities to destroy our enemies.

# Warning!!! Beware Of Thorns

It is God's plan that all things (good or bad) work together for the good of those who love the Lord and to those who are the called according to God's divine purpose. Remember, Samson had a purpose. Even though Samson had disobeyed God, God's purpose for him would still be fulfilled because of an established covenant.

God used the good and bad circumstances in Samson's life to complete his destiny. What the devil had meant for evil, God meant for the good of his people!

It is never good to disobey God's commands because the wages of sin is death. However, God used Samson's tragedy to carry out his purpose to overthrow the Philistines and to deliver Israel out of their hands.

Samson's disobedience led to him losing his strength, which had been sustained by the Nazirite vow to God. The cutting of Samson's hair negated his commitment in keeping the vow. As a result, he also lost his sight at the hands of the Philistines. Samson was blessed not to lose something much greater, his life.

When we sin in disobedience to God by stepping outside of our boundaries, we lose the strength of the anointing that sustains us. We fall out of fellowship with the Lord

# Taking Out The Trash

and in turn, we are unable to fight off the attacks of the enemy.

So, there is a price to pay for disobedience. Samson lost his sight. When we are disobedient, we lose the blessings that God has for us at that particular time in our life. The time and the season passes and we can never regain. Only by God's grace and mercy will He restore us.

As the story of Samson ended, while being held captive by the Philistines as a grinder in the prison, Samson's hair grew back. Samson was called to come forth by the Philistine lords to display his strength. Jesus, who was also prodded many times by the enemy, was tempted to display his anointing. The enemy insisted that Jesus turn the stones into bread to prove his Lordship. Jesus' response was that man shall not live by bread (man's source) alone but by every word that proceeds from the mouth of God (God's source which is His Word).

Then the blinded Samson was led out and positioned between the two pillars that supported the temple where the Philistines watched. Samson began to call upon the Lord to remember him. He prayed to be strengthened again in order to have vengeance upon the Philistines for his eyesight. Samson braced the two middle pillars and

## Warning!!! Beware Of Thorns

began to push with all his might and the temple fell on the lords and all the people who were in it.

So even at his death, God's purpose for Samson remained and was fulfilled to deliver the children of Israel from under the bonds of the Philistines.

Like Samson, Randy has a purpose for his life. Even as a little boy, Randy sensed he was destined for greatness. God had a plan for his life even before birth. Unfortunately, the devil also has a plan of destruction set in place to destroy Randy's life. The Lord insists that we must choose "this day" whom we will serve. God knows from the beginning the end. The end destination is already set in place and we must walk it out from the beginning.

God's purpose for us is to glorify Him. We cannot lose sight of our commitment or vow to God. We must never compromise our eternal relationship with Jesus Christ for a few temporary moments of pleasure.

On the other hand, Jade, who walks out the life of Delilah, has not realized God's purpose for her life and continues to walk outside of the will of God. The thorns in Jade's life and in her heart have choked out the Word of God.

# Taking Out The Trash

In the parable of the sower, the seeds (the Word) which fell among thorn bushes were choked out by the cares and pleasures of the world, along with the deceitfulness of riches. The condition of the heart (soil) is most important. Jade's heart is not conditioned to receive the Word (seed). Jade's heart is overshadowed with the trash (thorns) of selfish desires for sex and material pleasures, as with Delilah, who accepted money from the Philistines in exchange for the secret to Samson's strength. The temporal things in life can choke out the absolute essential things, which can bring eternal life.

This thorn of fornication has become as comfortable to Jade as putting on a pair of shoes in order to feel fully dressed. The times when God was trying to speak to her, the cares of the world and the deceitfulness of riches choked the Word out. She didn't want to retain the Word in her heart because it would bring conviction, and ultimately bring change. Jade felt so secure in herself and her possessions. She did not feel a need for a full-time Savior because life seemed to be going so well. So, in her mind, she had to be doing something right.

The point is that the deceitfulness of riches chokes out God. You do not feel subject to God's word because of the security you have placed in the riches. Jade made the

## Warning!!! Beware Of Thorns

material things in life her god, but the Lord insists that there shall be no other gods before Him.

> *(Exodus 20:3-6) "You shall have no other gods before Me. "You shall not make for yourself any carved image, or any likeness of anything that is in heaven above, or that is in the earth beneath, or that is in the water under the earth; "you shall not bow down to them nor serve them. For I, the Lord your God, am a jealous God, visiting the iniquity of the fathers on the children to the third and fourth generations of those who hate Me, "but showing mercy to thousands, to those who love Me and keep My commandments."*

Salvation comes as a result of choosing the one true God who is Jesus Christ. The Apostle Paul's heart desire for Israel was for them to be saved and to have a zeal for God but not according to their own "knowledge" about right standing with God. For it is with the heart that one believes and receives righteousness and with the mouth that one's confession is made to salvation. Salvation becomes the doorway to a changed heart and a changed mind.

Until the Word is deposited into Jade's heart and becomes a part of her, she will continue to submit to the cares and pleasures of life. Submission to God is receiving His Holy

# Taking Out The Trash

Spirit and trusting in His true riches. God's true riches are eternal and not the temporary pleasures of this world. The seed (Word) that fell among thorns are the ones who heard the Word but the cares, riches and pleasures of life choked the Word out.

How can Jade receive this richness of Jesus Christ? By desiring His absolute presence in her life, the condition of Jade's heart can be changed. The change has to begin with salvation. Salvation is the desire for the heart of God and the acceptance of God's will. One of the greatest Proverbs tells us that as a man *thinks* in his heart, so (is) he. So when the thoughts of the heart are of God, our life will project the will of His heart.

One definition of "think" is to bring about a given condition through mental preoccupation. This means that a given condition can be created by the mental preoccupation of thoughts. In essence, one's persistent thought process can give rise to his or her given condition, mode or state of being. The longer a worthless thought remains in the conscious mind, it then goes into the subconscious mind and shapes the condition of the heart. It then becomes the nature of the heart.

What is the remedy? Persistent Godly thoughts will result in having a heart with God's nature. So, the way we think

## Warning!!! Beware Of Thorns

in our heart or the way we respond in our flesh can lead us. As a result of the flesh, it will only lead us to destruction but a heart after God will lead us to Godly actions and reactions.

When Jesus is accepted as your personal Savior, the Holy Spirit comes to dwell within you. He forgives you of all your sins and begins to take out the trash (thorns). Salvation is the catalyst for change.

The God-like spirit of a changed heart begins the process of a renewed mind. Now, there is truly no condemnation to those who are in Christ and to those who do not walk according to the flesh, but according to the Spirit.

To be controlled by our fleshly desires is death and to be controlled by the Spirit is life. When our flesh controls us, it is impossible to please God. The flesh (carnal man) is an enemy of God. No flesh shall have glory in the Lord's presence but the devil does glory in our flesh.

> *(Romans 8:5-7) "For those who live according to the flesh set their minds on the things of the flesh, but those who live according to the Spirit, the things of the Spirit. For to be carnally minded is death, but to be spiritually minded is life and peace. Because the carnal mind is enmity against*

# Taking Out The Trash

*God; for it is not subject to the law of God, nor indeed can be."*

*(Roman 8:8-10) "So then, those who are in the flesh cannot please God. But you are not in the flesh but in the Spirit, if indeed the Spirit of God dwells in you. Now if anyone does not have the Spirit of Christ, he is not His. And if Christ is in you, the body is dead because of sin, but the Spirit is life because of righteousness."*

*(Romans 8:13,14) "For if you live according to the flesh you will die; but if by the Spirit you put to death the deeds of the body, you will live. For as many as are led by the Spirit of God, these are sons of God."*

Because the flesh demands to be satisfied, a war exists. The Apostle Paul said, "All things are lawful or permissible but he would not be under the power of, or controlled by anything." Sexual intimacy is good because God created it.

The first book of the Bible, Genesis, tells us that God had seen everything he made, and indeed it was good. The act of sex is binding between two people. When two individuals join their bodies together sexually, they actually become one. The two become one flesh.

## Warning!!! Beware Of Thorns

The same truth holds outside the confines of marriage. In simple terms, if you join your body with a prostitute, you become one with her or him. The great part and the intent is that if you join your body with your spouse (husband or wife) you become one with him or her. The greatest part is that if you join yourself with the Lord, Jesus Christ, you become spiritually one with Him.

> *(1Corinthians 6:15-17) "Do you not know that your bodies are members of Christ? Shall I then take the members of Christ and make them members of a harlot? Certainly not!"*
> *"Or do you not know that he who is joined to a harlot is one body with her? For "The two," He says, "shall become one flesh." But he who is joined to the Lord is one spirit with Him."*

Your body is a part of the body of Christ. It is a temple of the Holy Spirit. So, as singles and as Christians, we should submit our bodies to the Glory of God and turn away from sexual immorality. We can begin by taking out the trash.

> *(1Corinthians 6:13) "Foods for the stomach and the stomach for foods, but God will destroy both it and them. Now the body is not for sexual immorality but for the Lord, and the Lord for the body."*

Our bodies do not belong to us because we have been

## Taking Out The Trash

bought at a price with the blood of Jesus! Therefore, our bodies and our spirits must glorify the one who has redeemed us.

We can make a conscious choice not to walk on trashy ground with the enemy but to walk on Holy ground with Jesus Christ. Remember, life is about choices and the consequences that are associated with those choices. *"Therefore, if anyone is in Christ, he is a new creation; old things have passed away; and behold, all things have become new." (2 Cor. 5:17)*

We cannot continue to operate as the world does. We, the body of Christ, are now set apart from the world, which lusts after the fulfillment of the flesh. Galatians 5:17 says, *"For the flesh lusts against the Spirit, and the Spirit against the flesh; and these are contrary to one another, so that you do not do the things that you wish."* In other words, as a Christian, we cannot do what the flesh want and when the flesh feels like it. As Paul indicated, all things are permissible but not all things are edifying to the body of Christ, so take out the trash.

To live a "freewill" lifestyle is deception. Deception often takes place when we lack self-control. Deception is one of satan's most powerful weapons. So many times, we make

## Warning!!! Beware Of Thorns

excuses. One of the more commonly used is that men will be men and they cannot control their sexual desires, and men cannot go (without sex) as long as women can. A man may not be able to control his sexual desires, but what he can control is his response to his desires.

Even some women find themselves proclaiming that if they don't use it, they'll lose it. Well, if that were true, then God's word would be a lie, an untruth. This would make God, himself a lie. But because He has promised to perfect those things which concern us, we are assured that He is not a man who can lie.

When we accept Jesus Christ as our personal Savior and become born-again Christians, we take off the old and put on the new. We are now new creations in Christ. We remove the old wardrobe (fleshly ways) and replace it with a new wardrobe (spiritual renewing). Ephesians instructs us to put off the things concerning our former conduct and the deceitful lust of the old man. We are to put on the new man who is renewed in the spirit of his mind and is created according to the righteousness and true holiness of God. The new man changes the way he thinks about God and about himself. The renewed man has allowed God to take out the trash.

# Taking Out The Trash

The deception is thinking that it is okay to have sexual relations with someone to whom we are not married. The excuses used as justification are deceitful tricks of the enemy and are evidence of the corrupt "old man." These tactics are used to keep us from walking in righteousness and truth holiness. They are used to destroy relationships and to keep us from living in step with God's perfect will.

There is a price for disobeying God's word. The price may not be much to some. It may only cost you, your life.

**Allowing sin to govern our lives sells us out as a commodity to the devil to use as he pleases.**

When God gave Jesus Christ, who is His only begotten son, as a sacrifice, He bought us back for a far greater price. Therefore, our bodies belong to God. We are the redeemed of the Lord. The old sinful nature is no more because Jesus Christ paid the price for our sins so that in Him we might become new.

Wisdom comes by not submitting to the world's standards, which operate in darkness and corruption. As a new creation in Christ, the new man no longer walks as the rest of the world does. You are in this world but not of it.

## Warning!!! Beware Of Thorns

*(Ephesians 5:1) "Therefore be followers of God as dear children."*

*(Ephesians 5:3) "But fornication and all uncleanness or covetousness, let it not even be named among you, as it is fitting for saints."*

*(Ephesians 5:5-11) "For this you know, that no fornicator, unclean person, nor covetous man, who is an idolater, has any inheritance in the kingdom of Christ and God. Let no one deceive you with empty words, for because of these things the wrath of God comes upon the sons of disobedience. Therefore do not be partakers with them. For you were once in darkness, but now you are light in the Lord. Walk as children of light (for the fruit of the Spirit is in all goodness, righteousness, and truth), proving what is acceptable to the Lord. And have no fellowship with the unfruitful works of darkness, but rather expose them."*

*(Ephesians 5:15-17) "See then that you walk circumspectly, not as fools but as wise, redeeming the time, because the days are evil. Therefore do not be unwise, but understand what the will of the Lord is."*

The truth is that God placed within each of us passions and desires, but now as born again Christians, we are able to control them by not submitting to the flesh. We can now operate in the fruit of the spirit which is love,

## Taking Out The Trash

joy, peace, longsuffering, kindness, goodness, fruitfulness, gentleness, and self control because there is no law against these things. And those who belong to Christ have crucified (put to death) the flesh with its passions and desires.

Man or woman, you must have temperance (self control). You must bring your body unto subjection to the Spirit. Your flesh can no longer dictate the course of your actions.

**Your self-discipline in your flesh will imitate your self-discipline or submission to Christ in the spirit!**

Self-control or temperance is so important. You have become a new man or woman in God's eyes. God has restored to you a virgin spirit. Remember all old things have passed away, behold all things are new. You no longer act as a "sinner" because the corrupt man no longer exists. Your life is no longer dictated by the world's standards. You have chosen to stay within the set boundaries, which is God's will for your life. To step outside of the limits means to step into compromise or surrender.

> *(Romans 12:2) "And do not be conformed to this world, but be transformed by the renewing of your mind, that you may prove what is that good and acceptable and perfect will of God."*

## Warning!!! Beware Of Thorns

We, the body of Christ, have been washed by the Word and cleansed by the blood of Jesus Christ, the Anointed One and His anointing. Our sins are forgiven through the blood of the Lamb. Jesus has begun the cleansing by *taking out the trash*.

Trash is worthless to God but satan values worthless things. The worthless things that we open up our hearts to are the very things that close God out. If satan values worthless things, then surely Jesus Christ must value the worthwhile things.

So, why waste another day trying to consume things of no value? Allow Jesus Christ to take out the trash and replace it with hope, peace, joy and fulfillment. My intent is to make you aware of your options because we have a choice between an abundant life or just life. We must choose this day whom we will serve! The good part is that we don't have to wait for some drastic change to take place in our lives.

There may be someone who is reading this book at this very moment who thinks that he or she has to change his or her life completely around before accepting Jesus Christ as their personal Savior. Because you have swayed away from God, you may feel hypocritical. Well, Jesus loves you

# Taking Out The Trash

anyway. Why? Because He made you and He knows all about your wants and desires. He knows all the things you need and has promised to supply all of your needs according to the riches in Christ Jesus.

Jesus Christ is just the kind of merciful Father, who will accept you right now, just the way you are. He will accept you, even as the sinner you may or may not be and begin a new thing within your heart.

You are probably saying to yourself, "what is Jesus waiting for because I am ready?" Well, He's waiting for you to say "yes" to Him. He's waiting for you to confess with your mouth that "He is Lord and that He died on the cross for the remission of my sins, which have been completely washed away by His blood, and on the third day He rose, so that I would have life, eternal life."

You see it's just that simple to begin receiving an abundant life through salvation. Salvation is God's gift through Jesus Christ, which offers to us forgiveness of sins and protection from the destroyer. This gift of salvation that is given by God is not the result of anything we can do or cause. It is just what it is, a gift. When a gift is given, we have the opportunity to receive it. Right now, you can receive your gift by receiving Jesus Christ.

## Warning!!! Beware Of Thorns

> "AND YOU [He made alive], when you were dead (slain) by [your] trespasses and sins. In which at one time you walked [habitually]. You were following the course and fashion of this world [were under the sway of the tendency of this present age], following the prince of the power of the air. [You were obedient to and under the control of] the [demon] spirit that still constantly works in the sons of disobedience [the careless, the rebellious, and the unbelieving, who go against the purposes of God].
> Among these we as well as you once lived and conducted ourselves in the passions of our flesh [our behavior governed by our corrupt and sensual nature], obeying the impulses of the flesh and the thoughts of the mind [our cravings dictated by our senses and our dark imaginings]. We were then by nature children of [God's] wrath and heirs of [His] indignation, like the rest of mankind." (Eph. 2:1-3) (AMP)

We are in this world but not of this world.

> "But God—so rich is He in His mercy! Because of and in order to satisfy the great and wonderful and intense love with which He loved us,
> Even when we were dead (slain) by [our own] shortcomings and trespasses, He made us alive together in fellowship and in union with Christ; [He gave us the very life of Christ Himself, the same new life with which He quicken Him, for] it is by grace (His favor and mercy which you did

## Taking Out The Trash

> *not deserve) that you are saved (delivered from judgment and made partakers of Christ's salvation). And He raised us up together with Him and made us sit down together [giving us joint seating with Him] in the heavenly sphere [by virtue of our being] in Christ Jesus (the Messiah, the Anointed One)." (Eph. 2:4-6) (AMP)*

We are saved by God's grace through faith.

> *"He did this in that He might clearly demonstrate through the ages to come the immeasurable (limitless, surpassing) riches of His free grace (His unmerited favor) in [His] kindness and goodness of heart toward us in Christ Jesus. For it is by free grace (God's unmerited favor) that you are saved (delivered from judgment and partakers of Christ's salvation) through [your] faith. And this [salvation] is not of yourselves [of your own doing, it came not through your own striving], but it is the gift of God"; (Eph. 2:7-8) (AMP)*

No one can earn what has been freely given.

> *"Not because of works [not the fulfillment of the Law's demands], lest any man should boast. [It is not the result of what anyone can possibly do, so no one can pride himself in it or take glory to himself].*
> *For we are God's [own] handiwork (His workmanship), recreated in Christ Jesus, [born*

## Warning!!! Beware Of Thorns

*anew] that we may do those good works which God predestined (planned beforehand) for us [taking paths which He prepared ahead of time], that we should walk in them [living the good life which He prearranged and made ready for us to live]." (Eph. 2:9-10) (AMP)*

We were created in God's image with purpose and destiny. Today, choose life by receiving the free gift, which is free to us but was very costly for Jesus Christ. He gave his life that we might have eternal life. Jesus became poor so that we might become rich in Him.

## Taking Out The Trash

# Food For Thought

- *The seeds that Fell Among The Thorns are those who hear but the cares, riches and pleasures of life choke the Word out.*

- *Has fornication or sexual perversion become a thorn in your life?*

- *Deception can rule a person's life and give reason to justify his or her actions.*

- *Carnal (worldly) minds think that achieving the "American Dream" is the result of right standing with God.*

- *Possessions can become our idol, which becomes our god.*

- *Selfishness breeds corruption and corruption leads to death.*

- *Sexual intimacy between two people creates a bonding of the bodies and the souls.*

- *The bond is formed through an agreement by decision in the (mind), to (will) to give one's feelings or sensibilities (emotions) to another.*

## Warning!!! Beware Of Thorns

- *Soul ties must be broken by the renouncing of the fragmented pieces and a reclaiming of wholeness through the Word of God.*

- *The enemy has no legal right to enter without an open door. We have to recognize the cause and renounce the curse.*

- *When we get outside of our set limits or someone crosses over those limits, this is a warning not to proceed.*

- *We should never compromise our eternal relationship with Jesus Christ for a few temporary moments of pleasure.*

- *The temporal things in life can choke out the absolute essential things, which can bring eternal life.*

- *Once the main source of power is shut off, all outlets become defective or of no use.*

- *All things are permissable but not all things are edifying to the body.*

- *Salvation is the desire for the heart of God and the acceptance of God's will.*

# Taking Out The Trash

# 7

# Some Fell On Good Ground

§

Do you believe that there is good in all people? How would you answer this question? Is it safe to say that deep within all people there is a desire to do what is right and good? If this was the original intent, what went wrong? What happened to this desire? Paul gave an account of his very own struggle with good and evil in the book of Romans. Most of us have experienced this same warfare between our natural man (flesh) and the spiritual man.

Paul greatly distinguished a difference between the spiritual man who wanted to do good and in the carnal man where evil was always present. The Bible indicates that the spiritual man is willing but the carnal (fleshly) man is weak.

# Taking Out The Trash

In Paul's own personal war, he confesses that for the good that he willed to do (in his spirit), that he did not do; but the evil he willed not to do (in his flesh) that he practiced. The desire was in his spirit (inward man) to do good, but evil was always present in his fleshly body.

Paul said that when he desired to do good, evil was always present with him. For a moment, what Paul seemed to have forgotten was that his spirit was willing but his flesh was indeed weak.

Our spirits are willing to align with the Spirit of God, but the flesh has a mind of its own. Because the two are at war, the flesh must be brought under submission to the Spirit. Paul's strategy was to buffet or discipline his body in order to bring it under subjection to his spirit.

So what happened to the desire to do good? Paul expressed his belief in that if I do what I will not to do (in my flesh), it is no longer I (my spirit man) who do it, but sin that dwells in me (my flesh). Paul began to see a principle that formulated a relationship between good and evil. There was a coexistence of good and evil within one. The presence of evil in the carnal man (flesh) dwelled in the same body with the spirit man, who willed to do good.

## Some Fell On Good Ground

In Romans, Paul discovered a law that evil was present with the one who willed to do good. But in spite of the very presence of evil, our hope is that Paul's true delight was in the law of God according to his inward man. So, his true heart's desire was for the good in God.

What happened with Paul then, and now with many of us, is that the inner man (spirit) knows what is good, but the natural man (flesh) is at battle with the spirit. Sin begins with a thought in the mind, and is birth out through the flesh. The constant sinful thoughts in the conscious mind overshadow and suppress the desire in the heart to do what is good. The natural reaction of the flesh is to line itself up with these thoughts and begin to act out what is taking place in the mind, which is sin and evil.

Paul said it this way, *"But I see another law in my members, warring against the law of my mind, and bringing me into captivity to the law of sin which is in my members." (Romans 7:23)*

Again, what Paul was saying is that the law of his mind tells him to be spiritual minded but the law of his members tells him to be carnal minded.

The longer a worthless thought or perception stays in the conscious mind, the greater the opportunity for a

# Taking Out The Trash

stronghold to set up. The battle begins here in the mind. This is why we are instructed to take every thought captive and bring it under subjection to the Spirit.

When a sinful thought lingers in the conscious mind, it then goes into the subconscious mind and creates the condition of the heart. Once the thought is in the heart, there is no longer a war, because what is in the heart you have become.

Whether good or evil, it becomes natural, or a part of your nature. What was once just a struggle in the mind with a conscious thought has now shaped the person you've become.

**The thoughts of the heart will project the character or nature of the person.**

For as a man thinks in his heart, he becomes that man. In order to have a heart that projects the character or nature of God, we must continue to change the way we think with a spiritual renewing!

> *(Ephesians 4:23,24) "and be renewed in the spirit of your mind, and that you put on the new man which was created according to God, in righteousness and true holiness."*

## Some Fell On Good Ground

*(Romans 8:5) "For those who live according to the flesh set their minds on the things of the flesh, but those who live according to the Spirit, the things of the Spirit."*

Even from the time of our early awareness as very small children, we are aware of the difference between right and wrong; good and evil. The conscious awareness arose in man in the Garden. The seed was planted with Adam and Eve.

In the beginning, man only knew what was good, because God made everything in the garden that was good. In Genesis, God made every tree to grow that was pleasant and good for food. He placed in the midst of the garden the tree of life and the tree of the knowledge of good and evil. But God commanded man to eat freely of every tree except the tree of the knowledge of good and evil. So, man only knew of God's good pleasures.

In chapter three of the book of Genesis, Adam and Eve became disobedient. They took of the forbidden tree and this caused their eyes to be opened. Their conscious awareness arose in them and they realized they were naked and uncovered. At this very moment, they became exposed to another world, a world of evil. They became aware of their choices of good and evil.

# Taking Out The Trash

As a result of Adam and Eve's fall, God began to speak prophetically of man. *"Then the Lord God said, "Behold, the man has become like one of Us, to know good and evil. And now, lest he put out his hand and take also of the tree of life, and eat, and live forever". (Gen. 3:22)* So, now man must make a conscious choice to choose life over death or good over evil!

Take for instance, Crystal who in spite of knowing what was right, did what was wrong. She became so sure about the wrong things that she would even pray to God to make them right. She often practiced doing the wrong things because they felt so right. Why did they feel so right? The deception had shaped the person she had become. There was no longer a struggle, because what was in her heart had become as natural to her as breathing.

The carnal man was determined to do just what he pleased, regardless of the consequences. Crystal was determined to be in control but in her determination not to be controlled, the enemy was in control through her flesh. The Bible says, *"Whoever has no rule over his own spirit Is like a city broken down, without walls." (Prov. 25:28)*

This means anything goes and there are no boundaries or set limits. The Bible also says, that a man's spirit sustains

## Some Fell On Good Ground

him in sickness or in an unsound condition. Sustain means to keep supplied with the necessities in order to confirm, or to keep in existence. The spirit must be fed with the Word of God to supply a man with the necessities to keep him in existence as a strong and stable man of God. A weak spirit has no rule or charge over the flesh! It is the spirit of a man who stands as guard over the city. When the spirit man becomes weak and falls down, the walls fall down and anything or anybody may enter into his city.

Crystal grew up with both of her parents. She had a great relationship with her mother. However, Crystal's father never showed her mom any appreciation and she hated him for that reason. Crystal saw her father verbally and physically abuse her mother. Because of his lack of respect, Crystal was determined to never allow anyone to rule over her nor would she ever allow anyone to treat her this way.

This seed of anger was sown into Crystal's heart as a young girl and it became evident in every other relationship she would encounter. As a result, she had this distorted idea of marriage, along with this inability to show love or to receive it. Crystal was unable to love, because she was never shown how to love, by her parents. So, she went about life not ever experiencing the true love of her parents. In spite of this, there was a deep desire for love

# Taking Out The Trash

but the anger and resentment that she harbored would not allow anyone to get too close.

As a result of the trash in Crystal's life, she pushed everyone away. But for many others, the hurts and disappointments in life may have just the opposite affect.

Some women, as well as men, may find themselves seeking out what was missing in their parental relationship through others.

Because the relationship with our parents can greatly affect our future reltionships with others, it is important to have a solid foundation established of what is a true and unconditional love.

A father's love is especially important for both male and female. When there are no basis or standards of true love established in our very first relationship, then there are no measures or indicators of true love in our future relationships. So, how can we measure what is real or true?

A father's love establishes the basis for unconditional love. His love also sets boundaries or limits for what is acceptable and non-acceptable.

## Some Fell On Good Ground

So the lack of love and affection from our parents can cause us to be drawn to others or can cause us to push them away.

Having come to the conclusion that she would never get married, Crystal found herself in relationships that only lasted short periods of time. Whenever a man would get too close, she immediately began to push him away. Early into her relationship with Derek, she began to reject him for the fear of being rejected.

Derek was a quiet, soft-spoken and well-mannered guy but his timing was entirely bad. Crystal's previous relationship had ended with more rejection, which just compounded the many other disappointments in her life. Unfortunately, Derek had to suffer the consequences of these many heartbreaks and this only added to his very own load of garbage.

Crystal met Derek at the end of a very devastating divorce. The betrayal of his ex-wife had also left him too with deeply embedded roots of rejection and bitterness. His trash was so deeply hidden, that Derek thought he was over the hurt and ready to move on. In actually, he was only an accident waiting to happen. What was the aftermath? A typical situation where two broken pieces from two separate

# Taking Out The Trash

broken pasts were trying to come together to make some sort of a complete future.

In reality, Derek's heart suffered severe internal bleeding. The surface appeared to be healed but deep down the bleeding persisted. The painful wounds were evident in Derek's conversations. He often spoke of his desire to remarry but refused to be taken advantage of again. Derek was certain to never completely trust anyone, especially after his ex-wife took everything in the house and left him with the wreath on the door that read, "Welcome." He thought, "Welcome to what, there's nothing left."

The hurts were still in Derek's heart but in his mind he was ready to move on to another commitment. Although in his perception of marriage, he would insist on being in control of all the finances. Everything he had prior to marriage would remain his, if by chance the marriage did not last.

Of course some things would be purchased together, except for the house. It would solely be in his name, so that upon departure, she would only take that which belonged to her. Unfortunately for Derek and his new bride, they were already destined for failure.

## Some Fell On Good Ground

What is the path for someone like Derek who has been saved by grace but who does not know how to work out his salvation on a daily basis? The Bible says, *"For as he thinks in his heart, so is he..." (Prov. 23:7)* This means for Derek that his thinking about himself, others and the institution of marriage has to change.

When the mind is renewed, the heart changes and the healing process begins. Derek's emotional healing will begin when he releases the past by forgiving himself and those who have caused him hurt. The healing process puts the broken pieces back together.

What is the foundation for building better relationships? The more we know about Jesus Christ, the more we can learn about ourselves and others. Derek has to come to know the truth about himself. Because we are made in God's likeness, we must begin to think like God and begin to do things God's way.

Many times the ideologies gained from childhood about the institution of marriage have been incorrectly defined or left undefined. When a few bad experiences are added to the recipe, the bread comes out unleavened. The brokenness continues in relationship after relationship. The key ingredient that is often missing is Jesus Christ

# Taking Out The Trash

*"Jesus said to him, "I am the way, the truth, and the life. No one comes to the Father except through Me." (John 14:6)* What is God saying? I am the way to truth in life. I am the way to truth about all things that concerns your life, including your relationships.

Jesus' promise is to perfect those things which concern us. Learning to trust God helps us to extend trust to others. The Word of God is truth and it brings truth to our lives. The Holy Spirit comes to comfort and to guide us into all truth about ourselves and about others.

Trusting others does not come easy for most people and neither did it for Crystal. One day she wanted to be with Derek. The next day, she would rather not be bothered. Her thought was to be the rejector rather than the rejected.

What about the times when you would speak of plans for Saturday night, when you knew it was only going to be just another "Blockbuster night." It was another opportunity to be the rejector. Not realizing the hurt it would cause the other person, the rejection was passed on. It made you feel better to know that for once, someone else was being rejected beside yourself.

The lesson here is that hurting people will hurt other

## Some Fell On Good Ground

people with what is believed to be valid reasoning. Our past hurts and disappointments lend to this reasoning.

Crystal knew there was something different about her because most people didn't quite understand her. She never had many friends, male or female. Because Crystal spent most of her time alone, there were many wondering thoughts as to why.

Crystal faced the same challenge that we all face and that is to be delivered from what people think about us. Sometimes the hardest task is to believe who God says that we are and not whom others may say we are. The words that we speak about others can bring life or destruction. Gossip can be somewhat of an effortless task with lasting effects. It can be a full-time job for some people, with no pay. Gossiping can become a part of our everyday conversations. The task becomes so effortless because it feels so natural to our flesh. Then it becomes a full time hobby rather than a task.

Falsely labeling people is cruel and destructive. This is one of satan's oldest tactics, which he uses to destroy many lives. To put it plain and simple, let's not allow satan to enlist us in his army because he is always looking for a few good men or women. He really has no preference and

# Taking Out The Trash

all that is required is a pair of willing and able-bodied lips.

So, what does God have to say about gossiping? The Bible refers to gossipers as busybodies who wander from house to house saying things they ought not.

Gossipers will be accountable to God for every word that is spoken out of their mouths. We should be cautious of our choice of words. With our mouth, we can speak either life or death to others and ourselves. James 3: 9-10 says, *"With it we bless our God and Father, and with it we curse men, who have been made in the similitude of God. Out of the same mouth proceed blessing and cursing. My brethren, these things ought not to be so."*

Remember that out of the abundance of our hearts, the mouth speaks. So let us only speak words of truth and blessings about others, and not destruction. Our words, whether good or bad, have great and lasting effects.

Crystal, who was disturbed by these rumors, began to really question why her relationships never lasted. Maybe, marriage would be the answer to all of her woes. But was there really something wrong with her? Billy didn't think

## Some Fell On Good Ground

so. He was an older divorcee who came with answers to all of her questions. Could he really be her answer to all the whispers and stares?

Crystal's rationalization would allow Billy to move in, so that everyone would know that she was okay. "Of course, it would only be for a little while until she could pay off some bills," so she thought.

As time passed, Crystal saw even more signs that the relationship was wrong but if she continued to pray to God, it would work out. Because everyone knows that God always hear a sincere prayer, and who could be more sincere than Crystal. If only she could get Billy to be more responsible and committed, maybe then he would make the ideal husband.

Crystal wasn't real sure why Billy was so afraid of commitment. But maybe it had something to do with him being forty-two and having lived at home with his mama since his divorce. This wouldn't be so bad except the divorce was final ten years ago. So Billy sought comfort in his relationship with Crystal because it provided him the same care and feel of his mother's house. And he really did seek commitment, not that of a wife but a mother.

# Taking Out The Trash

To no surprise, the relationship was short-lived. Billy moved on to find another place to lay his head, a place of comfort and convenience.

As for Crystal, Billy was now gone but the rumors and the thoughts of marriage still remained.

Crystal was so sure that God had spoken to her one night in a dream. So she began to plan for the big occasion. She immediately started to shop for the perfect dress. She thought to herself, "should I go formal or semi-formal? What color would look the best on me? White makes me look too round. Maybe, I should go with a pastel color. First, I have to decide on the invitations. What about the food? I know my family can really eat, so we need real food. I mean real food, like fried chicken. Mama always said the way to a man's heart is through his stomach. Okay, now that we have the menu all set, there is just one thing missing, but he's on the way."

As unreal as this may sound, the deception is very true. Deception can come in many different forms but it has only one source. Remember as a man thinks in his heart, he will become that man.

So, had Crystal's constant thoughts of marriage taken the form of a prophetic dream? Crystal had dreamed she was getting married. So sure of it, she began to prepare herself because she wanted to have everything just right when her answer appeared. So she announced the good news to all her friends.

But as time began to slip away and reality began to set in, Crystal saw the man of her dreams; marry someone else. Why had she looked for love in all the wrong places? Because it seemed as though God was not moving fast enough, Crystal's soul became very dissatisfied and it had a great desire for this connection.

Oftentimes, we miss God and our lives are played out in lies and deceit. Deceived by what she considered to be a confirmation from God, Crystal began to operate in that deception. Deception comes from satan who is the father of lies.

The desire for marriage was so strong and deep that the timing was just right. The loneliness, the rejection and confusion were the results of an unrenewed mind and a spirit that was disconnected from God. The tracks of marriage was played over and over in Crystal's mind so much that the fantasy seemed a reality. This deceit causes us to believe and live a lie.

# Taking Out The Trash

The battle begins in the mind. Here is where a stronghold of deception takes root. Once the thoughts are rehearsed over and over, the tracks go deeper and deeper and become the thoughts of the heart.

The spirit of deception is looking for a place to hide itself in darkness and what better place than Crystal's dreams (night watch). What was thought to be a confirmation from God was her very own manifested dream of deception.

> *(Jeremiah 29:8,9) "For thus says the LORD of hosts, the God of Israel:'Do not let your prophets and your diviners who are in your midst deceive you, nor listen to your dreams which you cause to be dreamed. 'For they prophesy falsely to you in My name; I have not sent them,' says the LORD."*

The Bible says the heart is deceitful above all things. God clearly examines the thoughts of our heart but so does the thief of darkness. What is your heart thinking about? Who have you become? What are your dreams prophesying to you?

The enemy's main objective is to deceive in any manner, in which he can. Whether imaginary thoughts, ungodly soul ties or desires, the enemy comes to steal, kill and destroy the devine plan that God has for your life.

## Some Fell On Good Ground

He wants to deprive us of truth and keep us disconnected from the one who is Truth.

God inspires true prophecy. It is a revelation of God's divine will. Prophecy may be in the form of a dream, vision or a spoken word that generally comes through a prophet. Prophecy will affirm and confirm God's will for your life. True prophecy comes from the heart of God as a confirmation to the heart of man. Because God is Spirit, prophecy connects to the spirit of man.

But for every truth in the Bible, the father of lies has a counterfeit. The counterfeit will prophesy falsely to the desires of your soul. In the very depths or dark places of the soul, there may be a strong desire for something or someone.

**And God will give you the desires of your "heart," not of your soul, when your delight is truly in Him.**

A counterfeit prophecy will prophesy to your soul, what it is already longing for, because the soul seeks a connection. The deception is a connection with a familiar spirit that is not the Spirit of God. There are certain demonic spirits assigned to individuals and families and their soul purpose is to deceive and destroy.

# Taking Out The Trash

The soul (mind, will and emotions) must be one with the spirit of man which seeks to be one with the Spirit of God. This creates a three-part harmony and the right connection. A satisfied soul greatly dislikes what is honeycombed with lies and deceit, but to a dissatisfied soul every bitter thing is sweet and seems to be the right connection.

There is something to be said of the old cliché, "an idle mind is a devil's workshop." And Spencer had the right tools for the job. He would tell Crystal all the things she wanted hear in one ear, while God was saying the things she needed to hear in her heart. Spencer was confident that all Crystal needed was a good man. So, he immediately began to pull her away from her support system and what she knew to be true. Her family and friends began to look like the enemy. Because it is always to the adversary's advantage to move us away from our covering and the people who support us, so he tries to bring division.

So, what was truly causing Crystal's uneasiness about her relationships with men? Why were people falsely accusing her? Crystal knew that there was something unusual about how she responded to men and even to some

## Some Fell On Good Ground

women. Oftentimes she would completely separate herself from both. She often felt this confusion from within. There always seemed to be this inner struggle to try and prove to others that she was ok.

Where did this tug of war come from? In the Old Testament of Proverbs, the scriptures tell that a curse does not come without a cause. There has to be a reason or cause for a curse. And the cause began even before Crystal was born.

Crystal was unaware of the open door that allowed this spirit of homosexuality to walk into her family's bloodline. The words spoken through the rumors allowed this ugly spirit to raise its head and try to attach itself to Crystal through the passing of generational curses.

Biblical scriptures warn us of bowing down to false gods. The Lord, who is a jealous God, visits the iniquities of the fathers on the children to the third and fourth generations. The crippling effects of the iniquities of our ancestral parents can flow down through three and four generations.

There are demonic spirits that have been assigned to specific families. They have been given the legal right to enter into a family's bloodline because of the presence of

# Taking Out The Trash

iniquity and sin. This is one way we can be affected by our parents' choices.

Crystal's grandmother had been forced to participate in homosexual acts as a young girl. Crystal was not a homosexual but there was a spirit of homosexuality in her family. This was the cause. This was the enemy's open door and his legal right. He tried to use this perverseness in the passing of generational curses to accuse Crystal of being someone who she was not.

This is a ploy of the enemy to kill, steal and destroy. He comes before God as the accuser of the brethren. But by the grace of God and His covering, Crystal did not respond to the temptation but the struggle to resist was there. Unfortunately, many do respond without any truth as to why.

There are many reasons why a person may get involved in homosexual relationships. Whether male or female, there is an open door that allowed the enemy to bring the deception. The door may have been opened in past generations. There may have been someone who voluntarily participated in homosexual acts or someone who may have been unwillingly raped or molested.

## Some Fell On Good Ground

Homosexual relationships may develop because of hurt or rejection by a male or female figure. The wounds become an open door to receive what is unnatural and is not ordained by God. A major point is that if the door has been opened, then you now have to completely close it. Oftentimes the tendency is to go back to what is familiar.

I once read a book by Shelia Cooley, "Why The Hymen." There were many truths given through great revelation. Cooley talked about how God made man to be headship of the body. The body is the woman. So, when two men are engaging in homosexual acts, there are now two heads with no body. It is deformed. The same truth applies to two women involved in homosexual relationships. Two bodies come together with no head. This is not the way God intended for it to be, because He is a God of order and purpose.

Proverbs 26: 2 says, *"Like a flitting sparrow, like a flying swallow, So a curse without a cause shall not alight."* There must be cause in order for a curse to come. There is a cause and an effect. The effects can pass from generation to generation until the cause is recognized and the door is shut.

<u>Resource</u>
Cooley, S. (1997). Why The Hymen.
    Tulsa, Oklahoma: Logos To Rhema Publishing.

## Taking Out The Trash

When we open the door, the enemy has the legal right to come in. Closing the door involves recognizing and acknowledging the curse, then it must be renounced. The next step is to reclaim the promises of God by speaking His word over your life daily. Galatians 3:13 says, *"Christ has redeemed us from the curse of the law, having become a curse for us (for it is written, "Cursed is everyone who hangs on a tree")."*

The Bible also instructs us to work out our salvation daily. It is a daily effort and choice to remain under the covering of the Almighty God by staying in His will.

The rumors, spoken about Crystal, were a response to a shadow that looked like the real thing. What does this mean? For example, a person has received a healing from cancer, which is a curse, but according to the x-rays, it appears that something is still there. But it is only a shadow trying to appear as real, because the curse was broken when the healing was received.

The rumors (words spoken) tried to reopen the door in Crystal's life and it was open just enough for a shadow to appear through. Remember, a shadow can only appear in form, because it has no life.

## Some Fell On Good Ground

When you know that God has healed and redeemed you from the curse, the enemy can only produce a shadow of death. Psalm 23 refers to it as the valley of the shadow of death. This is a place where we can fear no evil because thy rod and staff comfort us! Remember our words have power. They can either speak life or death to someone or a situation.

We must remember that by grace we have been saved and by grace we have been set free. The comfort to our hurts and pains cannot be found in man nor is man the answer. Because Jesus Christ has already suffered and died, He is the only answer.

Even at one of the lowest and loneliest moment in Crystal's life, a song began to speak to her heart. Over and over she began to hear a whisper of this little song which she had heard many times before. This song would ask God to open the eyes of her heart and allow her to see Him. If Crystal could truly see God then she could truly see herself in His image. She began to feel again what had been missing in her life and that was the presence of the Lord. Crystal then realized that she really did want to see Jesus for herself.

The Word of God began to speak to Crystal's heart through a song. Her faith increased again and she believed God

## Taking Out The Trash

even for her healing from Lupus. At the age of twenty-two, Crystal had been diagnosed with this medically-incurable disease.

She recalled how she had questioned God. What had she done to deserve such a horrible thing? For many years, she was angry with God and wanted Him to know. Fortunately, the seeds (Word) that were planted into Crystal's heart as a teenager growing up in church were being watered again. The seeds started to spring forth life through a song in Crystal's heart. Whatever was deep inside Crystal, began to resurface.

The Word of God will give life to the ones who hear and receive; and for Crystal, it meant life. The seeds that fell on good ground stand for those who hear the Word and retain it in a good and obedient heart. They keep the Word in their hearts (good ground) and persist until they produce fruit with patience. The Word is kept until it manifests itself into reality in the form of salvation, deliverance, healing and the many blessings of God.

Crystal began to renew her mind with the Word of God and she began to have a change of heart. The change in her life was gradual but she saw progress. Her thought process and her attitude towards life began to change.

## Some Fell On Good Ground

Crystal's confession of her sins and repentance allowed the Holy Spirit to come in and begin to take out the trash.

Crystal's temple (body, soul and spirit) was being washed with the Word and cleansed by the blood of Jesus Christ. She was now walking in the spirit and no longer in submission to her flesh.

Crystal was walking by faith and not by her sight. The anger and resentment that she harbored toward her father were now released. So, God could begin a complete healing and restoration in Crystal's life. All the trash that she took in as a child and while out of fellowship with God was taken out and replaced by the love of Jesus Christ. And this was evident by her emotional and physical healing.

Crystal spoke God's word over her life and into the lives of others. The power of the arm of the Lord had been revealed to Crystal and she had no doubt to be completely restored.

Healing is received when there is a revelation received about the power of God's word and His ability to heal. A revelation is the revealing of something not previously known. Healing begins on the inside, so it must first be received on the inside.

# Taking Out The Trash

A revelation has to be received in the spirit (heart) about God's healing power. Then the Word spoken will bring what is on the inside to the outside, and then healing will be manifested in the natural.

The Bible says, "Out of the abundance of heart the mouth speaks." God spoke what was already on the inside of Him into existence, and the earth was formed and was no longer without void. In Him was life, so He spoke out life. When the Word of God (seed) is received as a rhema word, it then has become life and it will produce after its own kind.

Because God is so faithful to perform His word, Crystal's confession that, "by Jesus' stripes I am healed" caused her (body, soul and spirit) to be completely healed by faith.

> *"But He was wounded for our transgressions, He was bruised for our iniquities; the chastisement for our peace was upon Him, and by His stripes we are healed." (Isaiah 53:5)*

God healed Crystal's physical body from sickness and all of the emotional and spiritual wounds from the past. By living and speaking God's word, God's presence and His anointing brought forth a complete restoration in Crystal's life. God began to restore everything that the devil had stolen and more.

## Some Fell On Good Ground

Jesus Christ's refining process will always bring a complete restoration of body, soul and spirit, when we allow Him to take out the trash.

Through prayer, reading and meditating in God's word on a daily basis, Crystal began to hear from God. God spoke to Crystal's heart and assured her that He always loved her in spite of anything she could ever do. God loved her so much, even when she did not love herself.

Because for so long Crystal did not love herself, it was impossible for her to love someone else? She realized that Jesus Christ was the missing piece in her puzzle. Now that she had found Him again, the puzzle was complete. Crystal knew that He was the man she needed to make her whole, because he would become to her everything and even more. This is why Jesus said, "call to Him and He will show you great and mighty things which you do not know."

When Crystal reconnected with Jesus Christ, her life was restored. Restoration came to her much like the Samaritan woman who met Jesus at the well. Like this woman, Crystal had encountered many disappointments in life. The Samaritan woman had five husbands and the man who she was presently with was not her husband.

## Taking Out The Trash

This woman would experience at least six broken relationships. From these relationships, she was left unfulfilled and rejected. Something was missing in her life and these men could not satisfy the constant yearn or thirst that needed to be filled. But truth was revealed to both the Samaritan woman and Crystal when they met Jesus, the seventh man. In the Bible the number seven represents completion and divine perfection. So when they met Jesus, they met fulfillment.

This very divine appointment with God began their healing process. It began the restoring of what was lost, which was life. That place of their greatest hunger and thirst (the soul) was satisfied.

The Samaritan woman had been seeking things and people, which could only bring a temporary sense of satisfaction and not a lifetime of fulfillment. This fulfillment can only come from meeting Jesus Christ right where you are. Once you come face to face, then you must recognize Him as Truth and began to admit truth. This sets the order for a relationship with the one who is Truth, Jesus Christ.

In this story of the Samaritan woman who met her Messiah, Jesus departed Judea on a journey to Galilee.

## Some Fell On Good Ground

The Bible emphasizes that Jesus needed to go through Samaria on his way to Galilee. This would indicate that there was a necessity or obligation for Jesus to go through Samaria. The assumption would be that there was a need to be met there.

On this journey, the story tells of the place where Jesus came to rest. Which interestingly is the very same place where Jacob's well was located. The well sat on a plot of ground that Jacob had given to his son Joseph.

The thirty-seventh chapter of Genesis spoke of a pit that Joseph had been thrown into by his jealous brothers. From that very moment, this plot of ground became a prophetic place of transition from one place in life to the next.

This well symbolized a turning point or place in the spirit for both Joseph and this Samaritan woman. Both were at a very dark and solitude place in their lives. Both had been rejected by those they assumed would love and receive them the most. Joseph was sold into slavery by his brother but later transitioned from the pit into a position of favor with those who held him captive. The Samaritan woman who was shunned by the women of her community became an outcast.

# Taking Out The Trash

For the Samaritan woman, light was shown even at her darkest moment. First, she met Jesus at this well. It was very necessary for Jesus to go through Samaria on his journey to Galilee. The necessity was for the fulfillment of the prophecy. The prophecy was that of God's divine will and it had established this well as a prophetic place of transitioning from one phase in life to the next. As a result of this woman's meeting with Jesus at this prophetic place, at that moment her life began to be transformed. Crystal would also find her life being transformed and transitioned from the pit to the palace.

In the process of transformation, Jesus tells the Samaritan woman to recognize who He is, and what He has to offer her, the free gift of everlasting life. Living water would be given to her and she would never hunger or thirst again. Thirdly, Jesus wanted the woman to be truthful to herself. The admission of sin in our lives recognizes the need for a Savior.

We must accept Jesus as our Savior and recognize Him as the only true God. The purification begins with the admitting of truth not only about Jesus but also about ourselves. The Samaritan woman's open admission, of not having a husband, was the doorway that allowed Jesus to come into her heart. Jesus was allowed to enter into her life, and began to take out the trash.

## Some Fell On Good Ground

Like this Samaritan woman, Crystal met Jesus, recognized Him as truth and admitted her brokenness. When we admit we are broken, then we can receive truth. Self-admission opens up the soul (mind, will and emotions) to allow truth (light) to come into the dark places. The truth is that darkness cannot stay where there is light.

Crystal's heart would now be ready and willing to receive God's word. Recall in the parable of the sower, the seeds that fell on good ground represent those who hear the message, and retain it in a good and obedient heart. They persist with patience until they produce fruit, some a hundredfold, some sixty, some thirty.

By seeking first the kingdom of God and His righteousness, Crystal saw that all those things that God had promised were being added to her life. There was no doubt in her mind that while God was preparing her, He was also preparing her a mate and at the right time (God's time) they would some day meet.

Crystal knew that obedience to God's word and patience were the keys to producing the potential hundredfold harvest. Crystal was not only reading the Word but she was becoming the Word. She was now becoming the Word that was in her heart. The desire to do the wrong things was no longer taking precedent in Crystal's life. She now

## Taking Out The Trash

walked in holiness because like Paul, her true desire was to please God. This does not mean she did everything right.

Crystal filled up her conscious mind with God's word and it was received down in her heart. Now every time the flesh wanted to do evil, the Word would bring conviction. Then Crystal made the choice to be led by the Spirit and not by her flesh.

The Holy Spirit speaks to our heart. Crystal's heart was filled with the Word of God and the flesh had to line up with what was in her heart. The trash of this world was no longer a part of Crystal's life because she knew the wages of sin would cost her a price she did not want to pay. Crystal was determined not to allow anything or anyone to cause her to fall out of fellowship with her Savior.

Crystal was now sanctified and empowered by the Holy Spirit. Sanctification means to make holy by setting apart for sacred use. Being set apart from the world and its standards empowered Crystal to operate in God's grace and His anointing. She willingly allowed God to take out the trash.

When God sanctifies you, man or woman, this may even mean to be set apart from people whom you may care for.

## Some Fell On Good Ground

If the other persons are not living according to God's word, they will not understand the things of God because they do not know God. Unfortunately, people and their ungodly persuasions can become a stronghold or hindrance in our relationship with Jesus Christ.

The subject of fornication has been addressed numerous times. This is a tactic that satan uses when he tries to convince us that it is okay to have sexual relationships outside of marriage. As a single person and as Christians, it is not the will of God to commit sexual immorality or fornication.

God placed within each of us seed that cannot be wasted. His seed is design to produce God promises in our lives. God's seed is holy and free from sexual immorality. His seed cannot be contaminated, so take out the trash.

Good seed will produce after its own kind and therefore, God commands His seed to be holy because He is Holy. By refusing to be obedient to God's command, you are rejecting the promises of God.

> *"For this is the will of God, your sanctification: that you should abstain from sexual immorality; that each of you should know how to possess his own vessel in sanctification and honor, not in passion of lust, like the Gentiles who do not know*

## Taking Out The Trash

*God; that no one should take advantage of and defraud his brother in this matter, because the Lord is the avenger of all such, as we also forewarned you and testified. For God did not call us to uncleanness, but in holiness. Therefore he who rejects this does not reject man, but God, who has also given us His Holy Spirit." (1 Thess. 4:3-6)*

The Bible says that obedience is better than sacrifice. So do as your Father has asked of you and take out the trash. Be obedient unto God who is your Father in heaven.

## Some Fell On Good Ground

## Food For Thought

- *The seeds that Fell On Good Ground are those who hear and retain the Word until they bear fruit with obedience and patience.*

- *Our spirits are willing to align with the Spirit of God, but the flesh has a mind of its own.*

- *We have to buffet or discipline the body to bring it unto subjection to the Spirit.*

- *Sin begins with a thought in the mind, and is birthed out through the flesh.*

- *Once the thought is in the heart, there is no longer a war because what is in the heart (good or evil), you have become.*

- *The thoughts of the heart will project the character or nature of the person.*

- *A weak spirit has no rule or charge over the flesh.*

- *It is the spirit of a man who stands as guard over the city. When the spirit is weak, the walls fall down and the enemy can enter in.*

- *Sometimes the hardest task is to believe who God says that we are and not whom others may say we are.*

# Taking Out The Trash

- *Gossipers will be accountable to God for every word that is spoken.*

- *Out of the abundance of the heart the mouth speaks.*

- *God clearly examines the thoughts of the heart, but so does the thief of darkness.*

- *Counterfeit prophecy will prophesy to your soul what it is already longing for because the soul seeks a connection.*

- *The deception is a connection with a familiar spirit that is not the Spirit of God.*

- *There are demonic spirits assigned to individuals and families and their soul purpose is to deceive and destroy.*

- *Once the door has been open to the demonic realm, you have to shut it by renouncing the curse and reclaiming the Spiritual Blessings of God through His Word.*

- *Healing begins on the inside, so it must first be received on the inside.*

- *God placed within each of us seed that cannot be wasted. His seed is designed to produce God promises.*

# 8
# A Single Vessel Of Honor

§

If I am single, then exactly what does that say about me? A single person is considered to be an unmarried person who is a separate unit or individual. What does it mean to be a separate unit and what is meant by individual? To be a separate unit means to be set apart from others or the whole.

When God desires to bring you into holiness and to purify you, then He must sanctify you by setting you apart for sacred use. The word individual characterizes one's own distinctive attributes or identifying traits.

# Taking Out The Trash

To begin the process of sanctification, God separates or sets you (the single person who is individually characterized) apart from some people or situations to make you holy. Holiness characterizes the individual and identifiable traits that mark the distinctions, between that which is secular (worldly) and you, whom God has set apart for sacred use.

If in God's eyes, to be single is to be separate or set apart from the whole for sacred use, then being single has great value to the Kingdom of God. Learning to become a satisfied single person involves being content in your present state as God has called you. In 1Corinthians 7:20, Paul said, *"Let each one remain in the same calling in which he was called."* If for the present time God has called you into singleness, seek to please God and to serve Him.

Remember that everything has a time and a season. Most times singleness is only for a season. It is a season of preparation and the making of a vessel of honor.

Why does God have you single? One reason is to commit yourself to serving Him and this will honor Him. When our attention is focused elsewhere, this causes a distraction from our commitment. The Apostle Paul encourages singleness because it has many advantages.

## A Single Vessel Of Honor

One advantage is the time to focus on building a relationship with Jesus Christ.

> *"But I want you to be without care. He who is unmarried cares for the things that belong to the Lord-how he may please the Lord. But he who is married cares about the things of the world-how he may please his wife. There is a difference between a wife and a virgin. The unmarried woman cares about the things of the Lord, that she may be holy both in body and in spirit. But she who is married cares about the things of the world-how she may please her husband. And this I say for your own profit, not that I may put a leash on you, but for what is proper, and that you may serve the Lord without distraction." (1 Cor. 7:32-35)*

It is important to remain focused on what God has called you to do and the person He has called you to become. God instructs us to be anxious for nothing but through prayer and supplication make our request known. The only way to know what purpose God has for you is to seek Him and allow Jesus Christ to be your main focus.

Relationships can be a distraction in your commitment to the Lord. A single person who is dating can encounter many stressful situations and diversions. Oftentimes committed single Christians try to make relationships work with others who do not have the same level of commitment to Jesus Christ. I believe we can be unequally yoked with unbelievers but also with believers who are less committed.

When someone knows who he or she is in Jesus Christ tries to have a relationship with someone who may not know Jesus Christ; this can create an unbalanced scale. The stress and anxiety caused by this type of relationship can be very distracting. Often the one who is committed to God becomes drawn away from Him. There is also a fear of offending the other person who does not have a personal or committed relationship with Jesus Christ.

When the Word of God is spoken by the one who is committed, it will always offend the person who has less of a commitment. Due to their lack of commitment and knowledge about God, there is usually a resistance to the Word. The offense is received because he or she often feels like they are being judged.

The conviction comes from the Word but is perceived as judgement from you. It is not the committed person who judges, but God, who is the Word. *"In the beginning was the Word, and the Word was with God, and the Word was God." (John 1:1)* This makes it very difficult to carry spiritual and edifying conversations with one another.

# A Single Vessel Of Honor

Relationships resulting from incompatibility can form feelings of oppression. Self-expression and free expression of your relationship with Jesus Christ become difficult. There is a problem because where there is no commitment, there is no relationship.

Another distraction caused by an unequally yoked relationship is that the person who is not committed to the Lord will not understand your commitment. He or she will require your time and attention and will view your commitment as selfishness. The constant reminder of your actions, regarded as selfish, will cause you to be unfocused. Rather than remaining focused on Jesus Christ and His will for your life, you become consumed with trying to change the other person into who you would like for him or her to become. Just remember the only person you can change is you and only with the help of the Holy Spirit.

We can see Paul's point that being married can be a distraction but also dating while single. So let us remain focused on what God has called us to be for this time. Which is to be single for a season and committed to Him. As a single person, you have less commitment to other things and more time to serve God. There is more time to become a complete and fulfilled person in Jesus Christ.

# Taking Out The Trash

Right now you can enjoy where you are and who you are. For most people, singleness only lasts for a season. Merely as a reminder, the Bible reads that for everything, there is a time and a season. If your desire is to be married, begin to sow seeds (the Word) into your life in this area.

I believe marriage is not a fifty-fifty relationship between two people. Marriage requires one hundred percent given by both individuals who are complete in Jesus Christ.

Yes, you may be single but not alone. Jesus is with you forever and always. He promises to never leave you nor forsake you. We can become vessels of honor when we are set apart for sacred use.

The only time to be concerned about a mate is in prayer time. In prayer make your request known to God, who will give you the desires of your heart! Plant a seed (the Word) and wait for the harvest.

## A Single Vessel Of Honor

## Food For Thought

- *Learning to become a satisfied single person involves being content in your present state.*

- *Everything has a time and a season. Most times singleness is only for a season.*

- *Through prayer and supplication make your request known to God.*

- *Relationships can become a distraction to your commitment to God.*

- *The only time to be concerned about a mate is in prayer time.*

# Taking Out The Trash

# 9

# A Dry Season

§

Sometimes we may go through what I would refer to as a dry season. It's a time when we may not feel anything positive or any progression in our lives. You can't seem to feel the presence of the Lord. This may be a time when you feel absolutely nothing spiritual. There is this emptiness inside and you know there is something missing. So like many of us, you begin to search, not knowing exactly what or who you are searching for.

Even though you have given your life to Jesus Christ and have accepted Him as your personal Savior, there is this little voice that's constantly saying; "You are not saved." Suddenly, you begin to think that maybe you are not really

## Taking Out The Trash

saved. This is what satan does so well, he comes to steal, kill and destroy the hope in you. This causes us to become unfocused and confused. We begin to take our eyes off Jesus Christ and start to doubt Him.

On the other hand, there is another still voice that is speaking to your heart and it's saying, "I need Jesus." Well, be encouraged because this is what Jesus wants. He wants you to need Him. Jesus wants you to come humbly before Him and say, "I need you Jesus." I need to feel your presence in my life."

Once we invite Jesus Christ into our lives, He promises to never leave us nor forsake us. Your relationship with Jesus Christ is not based on your feelings. It has absolutely nothing to do with what you are feeling. Your relationship with Him is not based on your emotions, because emotions change. One day you feel this way about something and the next day you feel another way.

The foundation of our personal relationship with Jesus Christ is built on faith. It is not a feeling. It is a knowing, a knowing that Jesus Christ has forgiven you of all your sins and He accepts and loves you, for you. So, be encouraged for God's blessings are with you. You may not be where you want to be but thank God you are not where you were. You are progressing spiritually. You are moving

## A Dry Season

forward in your walk with Jesus Christ. You are moving from glory to glory.

Could the reason be that we do not feel like we are moving forward in our walk with Jesus Christ is because He is carrying us? This reminds me of a scripture that encourages me, and assures me that Jesus is always near. Our Lord Jesus Christ does not move away, we do. He is always as close to us, as our heart and in our mouth.

> *(Romans 10:8) "But what does it say? "The word is near you, even in your mouth and in your heart" (that is, the word of faith which we preach)."*

Healing can even be received through a song. The words of a song ministered to my heart and assured me that Jesus is carrying me along, even when I feel that I can't go any further. The first time I heard this song, it followed a great Word from God that also ministered to me. The message emphasized the power of the cross and it reminded me that I am free—free from a life of sin and unrest. We are free from the hurts and the bruises of this life. So, we can rest in Jesus Christ because He is our peace. As the Bride of Christ, we must trust our Husband, who is Jesus.

Your walk with Jesus Christ is a daily walk. Inviting Him into your life causes a change to take place in you.

## Taking Out The Trash

The change may be gradual for some but it will come, if you do not give up. Jesus Christ encourages us not to be weary in well doing. This means not giving up on doing what is good, even if things are not going the way we would like at the moment. Because you do not faint and give up, your harvest will come.

If we can just hold on, Galatians 6:9 ensures us of God's promise, *"And let us not grow weary while doing good, for in due season we shall reap if we do not lose heart."*

We do not have to go through life collecting garbage while roaming around in the dark! Before your light goes out, you can receive revelation, release, and restoration by "Taking Out The Trash"!

> *"Let your light so shine before men that they may see your moral excellence and your praiseworthy, noble, and good deeds and recognize and honor and praise and glorify your Father Who is in heaven." (Matt. 5:16) (AMP)*

# Conclusion

§

My prayer is that this book has been insightful and at the least thought provoking for those who desire to live in the abundant life that is promised to us.

It was the Apostle Paul who said, "that all things are permissible but not all things are edifying to the body." You have the right to make the choice but there are others who may experience the consequence. So what happens to their right to choose? Remember that nothing just happens! There is always a cause and effect.

Someone once said to me, "that we sometime give the devil too much credit" and many times this is very true. But the real tragedy would be not to give him enough credit

## Taking Out The Trash

out of ignorance. This was evident in the charge spoken against the children of Israel through Hosea - "my people are destroyed for a lack of knowledge." The more we know the better choices we can make.

KNOWLEDGE is liberating but WISDOM applied is continuous freedom.

# Prayer of Salvation

*Lord, I accept you right now as my Personal Savior*
*I confess with my mouth, Jesus is Lord and believe in my heart that Jesus Christ died, and on the third day God raised Him from the dead.*

*Lord, I ask for forgiveness of all my sins and I thank you for your Son Jesus Christ who died on the cross for the remission of my sins.*

*Lord, I thank you for washing my sins away with the blood of Jesus who gives me a second chance. Holy Spirit I invite you into my life.*

*Lord from this day forth, I want to give my life completely to you. Lord, I pray your will for my life.*
*Lord you are the potter and I am the clay, mold me and shape me into whom you may. Amen.*

*(Romans 10:9-10) "that if you confess with your mouth the Lord Jesus and believe in your heart that God raised Him from the dead, you will be saved. For with the heart one believes to righteousness, and with the mouth confession is made to salvation."*
*(Romans 10:13) "For "whoever calls upon the name of the Lord shall be saved."*

# Prayer For Inner Healing

*Jesus, now that you are my Lord and Savior, I call upon you name.*

*I call upon the name of Jehovah-rophe, the God who heals.*

*I release all of the pain, the rejections, the many disappointments and I place them on the cross where you suffered and died in my place.*

*I receive your promised healing that says, 'by your stripes I am healed.'*

*I reclaim the resurrection power that raised Jesus Christ from the dead, and I know that same power gives me life and that is life more abundantly.*

*In the name of Jesus, Amen.*

# Acknowledgements

§

I would like to extend my greatest thanks to those who gave their countless efforts and prayers toward this project.

To Devie D. Perry, H. Faye Branch, Cheryl Smith, Gaye Cain and Karen Gittens, your labor shall not be in vain.

To Bobby Buchanan, Ernest & Maria Conyers, Janice Dowell, Merdis Buckley, Maria Torres, Tony Murdaugh and Danette Raffoul, thanks for the many prayers and encouragement.

A special thanks to those who saw God's hand and plan in this book and were inspired to endorse it. May the seeds that each of you have sown, return to you a hundredfold— Seed Time And Harvest.

As for my family, now that we all are older and our love has grown greater, our differences seem so much smaller. A big thanks goes to you.

*—Sharon*

# About The Author

The author (*s. y. shorter*) currently resides in the Dallas/Fort Worth area. Realizing now that it was not by chance, she would find herself in this southern region known as the "Bible Belt". She considers it a blessing to have the opportunity to partake of some of the most powerful and anointed ministries in the world. Divinely positioned here to receive great insight into the Word of God has brought personal healing and restoration to her body, soul, and spirit.

It is the author's intent to take the experiences shared in this book to challenge the readers to reflect on their own lives and find God in a way that will make them whole and healthy in all of their relationships. She gets to the core of some tough but common issues that many face in today's society.

The author's prayer is that this book will revolutionize your thinking about who you really are to the Lord Jesus Christ and your purpose in His Kingdom.

If you would like to contact the author for seminars or speaking engagements, you may do so at the following address:

Ready Writer Publishing
s. y. shorter
P. O. Box 4281
Irving, Texas 75015
or
syshorter@theimplantedword.org

# Thanks to the following business!!!

*For creative graphic designs:*
*Subclavian Grooves* (brochures, greeting cards, media covers etc.)
*Devie Perry*
*3512 Sydney St.*
*Ft. Worth, TX 76119*

subclaviangrooves@yahoo.com

*(817)714-4255*

*For special occasion gifts and baskets:*
*Creative Comforts*
*Speciality Items for the Bed & Bath*
*P. O. Box 1828*
*Hurst, TX 76053*
*Janice D. (817)284-2869*

# ORDER FORM

To order additional copies of Taking Out The Trash, complete the following information below.

*Ship to: (please print)*
Name _____
Address _____
City, State, Zip _____
Day phone _____

_____ no. of copies of Taking Out The Trash @ 13.95 ea.  $ _____

shipping & handling $ 3.00 per book  $ _____

5 or more books 20% discount (less discount) _____

amount enclosed  $ _____

*Make money order payable to*
***Ready Writer Publishing***
Send to: Ready Writer Publishing
s. y. shorter
P. O. Box 4281
Irving, Texas 75015
*writersinkpen@yahoo.com*